White Flash

Training with the RAF in South Africa in World
War Two

Ed: Dominic Butler

Original Author: John Noble

REF: 4559578
ISBN-13: 978-1494397715

JOHN NOBLE'S SERVICE

John's career in the RAF took him to many places throughout the war and even after, and below is a list of his various posts around the world. Details about each place are sketchy, and therefore have not been included in this book. It is an ambition to complete this one day.

Air Crew Receiving Centre, No. 3, St. John's Wood, London: 3/8/42 – 19/8/42

Air Crew Dispatch Centre, Brighton: 19/8/42 – 8/9/42

Air Control Centre, Ludlow: 8/9/42 – 30/9/42

17 Initial Training Wing, Scarborough: 30/9/42 – 4/3/43

11 Elementary Training School, Perth: 5/3/43 – 15/4/43

Air Crew Disposal Wing, Manchester: 30/4/43 – 16/5/43

Initial Flight Training School, Clairwood: 21/6/43 – 30/6/43

No. 2 Personnel Dispatch Centre: 1/7/43 – 17/7/43

No.3 Elementary Flight Training School, Wonderboom: 17/7/43 – 25/9/43

26 Air School, Peitersburg, South Africa: 26/9/43 – 18/2/44

43 Air School, Port Alfred, S.A.: 10/3/44 – 20/4/44

45 Air School, Oudtshoorn, S.A.: 20/4/44 – 27/6/45

Westlake, Capetown, S.A.: 28/6/45 – 30/6/45

Harrogate: 17/7/45

As you will read, John flew the Avro Anson, perhaps the most versatile training aircraft of the war. However, John first trained on De Havilland Tiger Moths, designed in the 1930's and operated by the RAF as its primary trainer. The Tiger Moth remained in service with the RAF until 1952 when many of the surplus aircraft entered civil operation.

Upon completion of a series of tests, John was moved onto the Airspeed Oxford, a twin-engine aircraft used to train aircrews in flying, navigation, radio-operating and bombing. The Oxford is low-wing cantilever monoplane with a semi-monocoque constructed fuselage and wooden tail unit. It had landing gear that is retractable into the engine nacelles and a tail-wheel. With a normal crew of three the seating could be changed to suit the training role. The cockpit had dual controls and two seats for a pilot and either a navigator or second pilot. When used as for bomb-aimer training the second set of controls were removed and the space was used for a prone bomb-aimer. When used as a navigation trainer the second seat is pushed back to line up with the chart table. In the rear is accommodation for a wireless operator facing aft on the starboard side. In the Oxford I a dorsal turret is located amidships.

Finally, John flew the Avro Anson, a British twin-engine, multi-role aircraft with the RAF, Fleet Air Arm and numerous other Commonwealth forces. It was the first RAF monoplane with a retractable undercarriage. This however, required no less than 140 turns of the hand crank by the pilot. To forgo this laborious process, Anson's often flew with the landing gear extended at the expense of 30 mph (50 km/h) of cruise speed. It was a relatively slow aircraft, with a top speed of 188mph and a service ceiling of 19,000 feet. However, it was loved by its crews for its simplicity and ease in the air.

On entering the RAF, crews would come from A.C.R.C centres, the most famous being St. John's Wood in London, where John was first posted. This was known as 'arsy tarsy' and there the transformation from civilian to a Cadet began. At A.C.R.C, men were given preliminary drill and a uniform, which was their introduction to service life. They would then be posted to an I.T.W. where they were to learn the basics of flying theory, service protocols, parade ground bashing and other monotonous duties that would make the boys into men. They would also be sorted out as to aircrew trades training, ranging from pilots, to navigators, to gunners.

After I.T.W, pilots would be posted to an E.F.T.S, and for John this was in South Africa under the 'The Scheme'. The Empire Training Plan, to give it its official title, sent pilots around the world to most of the Commonwealth countries for training. South Africa was under a parallel agreement, the Joint Air Training Scheme, where some of the pilots would stay with the South African Air Force and some would return to the RAF in Britain after months of laborious training.

After roughly 15 hours of attempting to make you into a pilot, men either flew solo or were 'scrubbed' and sent off to learn another trade. Many of these would serve as navigators or bomb aimers.

Forward

This is my grandfather's work. None of it is mine, not yet anyway. This is all his original work from the early 1950's, and is his story. There is no historical content so to speak of; he focused on his life, the space around him, and nothing else. I have done my best to add to this, and give it a bit more context in the massive subject that is the Second World War.

Before my grandfather passed away in December 2007, I took it upon myself to retype his memories that he had left me. He asked me to look after them before he died, knowing my fondness for history, especially military history. That is why this book exists – to me I am preserving his memory, something that has been so often forgotten for many other war veterans, whether there story is one of bravery, sacrifice or humour.

About John

John was born in Mexborough, Yorkshire, on 26th November, 1923 and died in Kettering on 12th December 2006.

His parents, Annie and Leslie, moved house a great many times, living in different parts of the country but mostly in Yorkshire. John and younger brother Geoff had very happy childhoods. Also Annie and Leslie both came from very large, close-knit families and the boys were never short of cousins their own age.

John had a job in a cinema up until joining the RAF in 1941, where he became a pilot, flying Avro Anson's amongst other things. John met Val while he was stationed with the RAF in South Africa in 1944, during the war. John had been posted to Val's home town to train pilots. They met in church and after the war Val came to England and she and John were married on October 19th 1946. They celebrated their Diamond wedding with a family party and a lovely card from Her Majesty the Queen. They had a lovely weekend break in Leeds – revisiting St. Matthews Church where they had married all those years before.

The couple lived in Leeds in a tiny flat where Anne was born in 1948, on June 21st. around that time John learnt that he had passed his final exam to qualify as an ophthalmic optician, following in the footsteps of his father Les. Later they moved to Weymouth, Dorset before moving to Dublin where Richard was born on September 16th 1954. By now Geoff was married to Sheila and they had a 6-year-old son, John. They also lived in Rathmines in Dublin, a short walk from Les and Annie and John and family.

When Richard was 6 weeks old John's family moved to a new home in

Barnsley, Yorkshire, where they lived for several years until a further promotion took them to Hanley in Stoke-on-Trent.

The final move was to Higham Ferrers in 1963 when John bought the practice in High Street, Rushden – where Argos is now situated. The practice was moved in 1970 to Church Street, Rushden where John had a long and successful business until his full retirement approximately 3 years ago.

John had four grandchildren, Charis, Simon, Kara and Dominic, and three great -grandchildren, Elliot, Jack and Caylum. Another great-grandchild is due in January. He also had two Nephews, John and David, and a niece Jane.

John loved to travel with Val and they went all over Europe, and to Canada and America. They have a lovely Spanish apartment and many happy holidays were spent there, the last one as recently as September this year.

John had a passion for film-making and was a very active member of the Rushden District Cine Club for around 40 years! He won many prizes for his Cine films.

John was also a talented painter and enjoyed being a member of Rushden-District Arts Society for a number of years.

John was many things to many people. Above all he was a kind, loving, generous family man. He was also a much respected ophthalmic optician, a talented film maker and painter.

His grand-daughter, my sister, wrote this passage for his funeral:
"Granddad John was the perfect grandfather, for many reasons. Not least because of his unswerving loyalty, unconditional support and interest in his grandchildren's lives, but also because of his ability to engage us in a variety of dangerous, mad and exciting activities over the years. I am so glad that we are children in a less PC age – a modern health and safety officer would have condemned the majority of his ideas as extremely unsafe and would have bound his hands a long time ago!"

"Many, many years ago, he introduced the family to a marvelous invention – indoor fireworks – which not only caused the asthmatic amongst us to choke whilst a cardboard clown puffed away on a cigarette, but also resulted in granddad dropping a lit sparkler on two year old Simon's toe! And let's not forget Granddad's version of the 'Firework Safety Code' – put all fireworks in a cardboard shoe box (normally without a lid) and if in doubt, do go back a few times and check the firework is lit. And make sure you use something inadequate to pin Catherine Wheels up with – so that your fence goes on fire. And always spend at least an hour the next day scouring the Castle Fields (and the Massom's garden) for empty firework shells."

9

"Granddad also taught us how to climb the biggest tree in the Castle Fields (after balancing on the narrow wall next to the stream) and how to sledge down the hills in extremely thin plastic sledges (with him in the back). He took us to Twycross Zoo, Wicksteed Park, The Fair and to Drayton Manor Park, going on all the rides with us (unlike our parents)"

"We also enjoyed eating at Grannie and Granddad's house because the pre-dinner arrangements were always fun and unusual – for example, hundreds and thousands sandwiches as starters, piling all the jam jars in the house up into a tower and trying to catch them when they fell and the wonderful drinks he introduced us to – not for Granddad the usual orange or ribena – no, we got a choice of: tonic water, bitter lemon, ginger beer, Russian (which usually accompanies vodka) and grenadine – all mixer drinks I might add!"

"Granddad had an extremely sweet tooth – something he passed on to his daughter and eldest granddaughter – is it any wonder our teeth are so bad! He loved most sweets (except acid flavours which made his neck hurt) and always had a bag or a box of something around the house – coconut mushrooms, jellied fruits, Pontefract cakes, chocolate orange peel, Black Magic, licorice torpedoes, sugar mice, licky licky, and Kendal Mint cake."

"We loved going on holiday with Granddad, whether it was meeting up with him in Spain, sailing on the QE2 or going on the blue train to Boulouris, I have never met anyone else who could (or would want to) swing two full buckets of sea water, round and round, like a windmill and not drop them. Or anyone who can make speedboats out of sand. Or create a family legend about a dead cat, whilst drinking endless bottles of Orangina. And who can forget the wonderful rubber dinghy's he brought us – how dangerous were they?! Granddad always filmed our holidays and other important events, which at the time was very embarrassing – particularly the kids from Fame, Kara and Simon, but what he did achieve was to create a wonderful archive of life in the 1970's and 80's – something which we are now extremely proud of and I certainly will be pleased to keep up the tradition and keep the memories alive with my camcorder."

"We always had great fun at Granddad's house; using making something – a noise or a mess mostly! He taught us how to mix Dragon's blood, how to dig potatoes, how to lift the lid on the drain and dig out Richard's old forgotten cars, how to throw Big Ted down the stairs (endlessly), where to hide in the airing cupboard, how to pull the enormous family sized crackers he brought every year, how to play the stylophone (joy!) and how to give each other dangerous wheelbarrow rides. Sadly, it seems that only Elliot has inherited his amazing artistic qualities – he did try extremely hard to teach each of us to paint, but it wasn't to be."

"We were especially proud to have a grandfather who was an optician and I loved the free pink plastic National Health Specs he used to bring me, when I was six. The Christmas parties at the shop were hot, loud and raucous but everyone still has fond memories of them. We also remember our journeys down to the pigsty (which is now the Peter Crisp Car Park) and watching Rushden Carnival out of the upstairs front window, trying to hit the worst floats with hundreds of half pennies Granddad enjoyed hording."

"Talking of hoarding – Granddad was the master – a skill which he has definitely to passed on to many of the family, particularly Anne! He loved to keep letters we had written, old programmes from shows I had been in, photos, old Disney film reels, clockwork toys, and a variety of other useful and interesting items. Alas, the only valuable things he did manage to throw away were two full sets of the Beatles autographs, for which Anne has never forgiven him!"

"I loved the way in which Granddad was keen to keep up to date with modern technology – he enjoyed having a mobile phone, even though he kept forgetting how to work it and he loved the idea of using a modern camcorder and digital camera. He also had a fondness for more modern TV programs, such as 'Phoenix Nights' and 'The Office' – which we all enjoyed discussing every Sunday."

This book has been published in John's memory, and for this brilliant family. I can take no credit for this work other than sitting down and typing my grandfather's words. I hope you enjoy his story.

Chapter One

The Corporal advanced heavily, and roared, "You are a clot!"

"Yes, Corporal" was the reply.

"What are you?"

"A clot, Corporal."

"Stand still when you speak to an N.C.O. Do it again!"

I did it again, and dropped the rifle. Stooping to pick it up, my hat fell off. The Corporal pounced, "Get fell out. Go and get your hair cut – at the DOUBLE!"

I doubled up the road, past hundreds of men on parade, all urging their eyes to do 180-degree turns, and took my place in the barber shop queue. I was a volunteer; I wore a white flash in my cap. I was an aircrew cadet, and my head had been shaved to the bone the day before.

"Your first flight," said the Flight Commander, "Will be familiarisation. You will take off, climb to 2,000 feet, and you pupils will then take over the controls flying straight and level. During the whole of your stay here you will be concerned only with simple flying – you will do twelve hours and will then be assessed on your ability. Some of you will go for further training as pilots, some as navigators, some as air bombers, and some as gunners." An ominous afterthought followed – "Some of you will be washed out."

A new intake, we were unfitted to fly from the main aerodrome, and consequently assembled on the parade ground with parachute and brand new kit. Boots were tucked beneath our flying suits or worn according to temperament. "Boots will be carried," boomed the corporal, "not worn. You're at Grading School, not Biggin Hill. And that goes for you with the suit-flying inner. Suit flying outers only. Understand?"

I respectfully carried my boots neatly folded beneath my suit flying outer. We were herded aboard a covered-in lorry, smuggled out of the camp before anyone of importance could discover our existence, and arrived at a satellite airfield some ten miles away. It had its own staff of instructors and mechanics, and a cookhouse, which was ran by civilians. Then I saw something and my heart sank; a Tiger Moth, a real aeroplane. This was it.

"Soon be up, now." Someone slapped me on the back.

"Wizard."

"Nice weather for flying," our Flight Gen Man remarked, "only two tenths cloud at about five thousand feet."

"Whacko"

"Nothing to flying those things," mused the sergeant.

"Good show."

"Yew lewk as though you're err-sick alreeeedy. What's up?" asked a Liverpudlian, pulling gently at his ripcord handle. I told him to get knotted; I was not in the mood for dealing with this Northern monkey.

We climbed from the lorry hugging our kit tightly, and assembled in an untidy heap, waiting for a corporal to appear. None came, and we straggled around, edging nearer to the aircraft until a sergeant walked over to us. He had his hands in his pockets, was without hat, and wore carpet slippers. He was a pilot. We relaxed. "Okay chaps. Canteen up." Taking advantage of this new atmosphere we unceremoniously dumped our kit, and walked round a hut towards the Mobile Canteen. This hut was occupied by a civilian girl who had a cardboard time-chart in her hand, poised over the amorous head of a Pilot Officer. "She's had it", said the Liverpudlian, but the rest of us pretended not to notice.

I was asking for some tea at the Canteen, when Gordon Graves sidled up to me, and whispered, "What do you think?" "About what?" I asked. He nodded towards the person who was handing out the tea. I saw what he meant, and slowly walked away from the Canteen. "Don't know, what do you reckon?" "Dunno" he sighed, "Have a look at the legs." "Good idea." I walked over to the Canteen again. But the girl, like all girls destined to spend the war years in Mobile Canteens, appeared to have no legs. I stood on tiptoe, trying to get a clearer view, until someone shouted, "Why not get inside?" The poor girl whipped round, and was so embarrassed that she pulled the shutters down and left. "Now we'll never know, eh John?" Gordon was right, for we never found out who she was.

The Flight Gen Man was the first to fly. "Hope his rabbits die, he'll have more duff gen than ever when he comes down." "I bet he goes solo in three hours", I quipped. We watched the instructor wave away the chocks, and taxi out towards the boundary in a zig-zag fashion. The plane took off, did a circuit of the airfield, and then flew off casually to do some straight and level. At first thought, it didn't look too bad. Besides, it was only our first trip, based on familiarisation.

A few more names were called, and gradually the little group of the uninitiated diminished. We kicked at stones, smoked incessantly, and tried to appear casual and nonchalant. But the waiting increased our nervousness and magnified the whole thing until one would have sworn we were awaiting our execution with a masochistic desire to 'get it over with'.

Three aircraft landed almost at once, and three pupils strode from the cockpits, jumping to the ground as though they had been flying all their lives. They ignored us with the same aloofness. But I didn't have time to care, because then I heard my name called. An instructor walked towards us. "SIR!" I shrieked. "You won't be flying today. Go give them a hand in the cookhouse, will you?" He strode away singing 'Rock of Ages' whilst I was left fuming.

I meandered towards the cookhouse, and a large lady, who seemed both serviceable and hygienic, hailed me. "Which do you want laddie, stew or prunes?" She indicated to two large pots. I lifted the lid of each and jokingly asked "Which is which?" Her reply was certainly not becoming of a female. I was then given a ladle and turning, informed Mildred in the bowels of the earth that she 'was on the stew, and how many prunes?' to which the incoherent reply translated into three per person with some juice.

I stood gallantly serving the prunes, becoming increasingly unpopular. To a man they hated prunes, and told me so, adding that I should be held responsible for any dire consequences that may result due to their consumption of them. I stood my ground and went on serving, until my grudge against society had been avenged, and the last man had been served. I told the formidable lady that I would now appreciate my release. She gave me some stew, and whispered, "Take four prunes for yourself." I scowled at her.

I sat next to Gordon Graves. "Struth, John, your asking for trouble!" he exclaimed, looking at my plate. I had taken eight prunes, and I still think that I was the only person in the RAF that liked them. "It's ok; I'm not flying until tomorrow."

I was wrong. A gale was raging the following day, and no-one flew. We were still smuggled out of the camp to the satellite, despite this. The aircraft were pegged down, and they creaked and groaned in the wind. We sat in the lorry until the instructors told the driver to go away as they were busy. We were whisked back to the main camp, and locked in the cinema. It was about half an hour before a diversion had been organized for us. The M.O. gave us an entertaining little lecture on the perils of smiling at the females at the town nearby, and indicated that, during our short stay in the vicinity we should one and all be tempted by the wickedest lot of females this side of the Equator. Quite a place, we reckoned. He then told us with fiendish delight what exactly would happen, having succumbed to temptation. We would lose all honour; it seemed, within minutes of leaving the camp gates. "He must have a share in the NAAFI" someone whispered. I didn't reply, he was an angry man.

As a complete change we were then shown a film on the same subject, during which, to our delight, the Flight Gen man fainted. After the film the M.O. told us with a sneer that if we wished to indulge in another obnoxious habit we may smoke, and then he opened all the windows. We smoked quite a few.

I asked Gordon about his flight the day before. He seemed quite satisfied with himself, but could tell me nothing that I considered useful. "The landing'll get me," he quipped, "Straight and level's easy enough. Who's your instructor?" I told him I didn't know. "Mine's Reynolds. F.O. Canadian. Hums into the intercom. They all seem O.K. except for F.O.

Burlingford. He's a foul-mouthed B******d, I'm told. Old Fred had him!"
Gordon looked round for Fred, spied him a few rows back and shouted to
him. But the lights when down and Gordon muttered, "Proper swine, Fred
says. He's sure to wash him out." From that point on, I had an uneasy
feeling that F.O. Burlingford would be my instructor as well as Fred's.

The two Tiger Moths, Light yellow in colour, and glinting in the sun,
neatly collided on the far side of the aerodrome. They locked together and
fell the last hundred feet in an obscene and terrifying embrace. A quiet
crunch rolled toward the Flight hut. The mobile canteen bun stuck in my
throat, my scalp prickled, and my knees buckled. I looked around to see if
anyone else had seen the accident. They all had, and no-one moved. Then, a
dozen dashing figures made for the alarm bell. It was a foot from me, so I
grabbed it and clanged it furiously.

A Jeep and ambulance raced across the aerodrome towards the settling
scrap heap from which a wing pointed incongruously towards the sky. A
few tiny figures hurried around, were lost to sight, and re-appeared again. A
slumped airman was cut from his harness. And then the ambulance and
jeep returned, driving toward the town at monstrous speed.

Two instructors climbed out of the Jeep. "A goddamn mess," said F/O
Reynolds, the Canadian, "blood all over the place." "Bull," said the other,
the Sergeant who had welcomed us on the first day, "they'll be alright." A
voice roared into my ear. "Righto – clot. You can stop ringing that thing
now. Get your 'chute, and come with me."

I blinked at F/O Burlingford, and then at the Tiger Moth standing ready,
in charge of a leering mechanic. I looked across the aerodrome at the
discarded wrecks, forgotten like broken toys. "Yes, sir." I murmured.

Chapter Two

"Let's go ice skating in Dundee" said Gordon. I shook my head. "No cashee, no washee." I said. "You go." "Look," said Gordon, "you don't need all that much money. I know a wangle. This is the only S.O.P. that we'll get here, so let's make the most of it. Train fare you can count as nil – its half price for forces at the Ice rink, and we can stay in the Y.M." "Train fare nil?" I argued. Gordon tapped his nose. "I know a wangle." He repeated. "Fit?" I said nothing. "What are you going to do then?" he asked. "Oh, going to the Christian Science Reading Room---" "Good god, what a way to spend an S.O.P!"

I saw his point, so I went to Dundee. His wangle on the railway worked. We walked through the Parcels Office at Perth, trying to look nonchalant, and as though we were looking for something, and no-one challenged us. We boarded the train, found an empty compartment, and sat down. I felt relieved, and Gordon felt jubilant. "See" he said, "not even a penny for a platform ticket. Now, if an Inspector gets on, all we do is buy a ticket from him, but that doesn't happen that often. You can travel first this way if you like."

"No thanks, this is bad enough. What happens at the other end?" "Dunno," said Gordon, dreamily, "I've never been to Dundee!"

When the train drew into the station, we made for the barrier. "Follow me" said Gordon, and went up to the ticket collector. "This isn't the train for Edinburgh, is it?" he asked. The collector, without looking at him, nodded. "Aye." "Hell, our kit!!" cried Gordon, as he rushed through the barrier. I followed on his heels, avoiding the eye of the Corporal who was trying to get in. "There you are. Simple, isn't it?" Gordon bragged, when he finally caught his breath. "I don't know whether it's worth it for four and six" I said. "It is if you don't have four and six."

I saw his point, so we began walking towards the town, looking for the familiar and comforting sign of "Forces Canteen", and eventually we found one down a side street. The air was thick with smoke, and there was a long queue for tea. In front of me stood a small soldier, in greatcoat, and a forage cap which had slipped over his eyes. He was swaying slightly, and now and again a vague smell of a farmyard wafted from him. He turned around, saw me, and rapidly focused his eyes. "Now we've all had it," he said, "the bloody air force is here." I ignored him and somebody told him to belt up as there were ladies present.

He turned to me again, but this time he was smiling. "What a shower" he said, and then he became confidential. "My brother's in your outfit. I tried to get in, but they wouldn't have me. Too little, an' I'm flatfooted. I am, you know. Flatfooted." He lifted his boot up. "There, what did I tell you? If it hadn't been for them I'd have been in the Air Force."

Gordon audibly thanked God for the man's flat feet, and ordered two teas. The drunken soldier floated across to us as we looked for a place to sit. He pulled a tube from his pocket. "Here, have a saccharine." He said, and gave us each a tablet, which we popped in the tea. I sipped mine. It tasted foul, and left a roughness on my tongue. I saw Gordon pull a wry face, and asked him what the matter was. "What filthy tea!" he joked, drinking some more.

Another soldier approached. "Hey," he said, in a rich north-country voice, "did 'e give you soom sackereens?" as he jerked his thumb. We nodded, and he burst out laughing. "You're a bugger, Bill" he shouted. Then, to all and sundry, he said "Bill's given these Air Force lads some of 'is sackereens! 'Aven't you, Bill?" There was a loud guffaw at this, and we began to wonder if we had perhaps been poisoned. "What are they?" I asked. "Them's tablets Bill takes to stop him smoking." The north-country man went on. "EE – joost you wait until you light up", and peeled off into hoots of laughter, in which all his mates joined in. Bill stood well hidden behind two burly Pioneer Corps men. "Come on, lets go" said Gordon.

We breathed deeply outside and the fresh air cut into us like a knife. "Let's get a bed, Gordon." I suggested. "They may all be filling up by this. As soon as we're fixed up, we'll come out again." He agreed, and we asked the way to the YMCA.

"Sorry lads," the Officer said, "we're full. Try the Church Army." This, too, was full. So were the Salvation Army hostel, and the Ladies Guild, and the forces club, and the last hostel of them all, the annexe to the Society for Fallen Women, was for women only and was full. "Wish I was a fallen woman" moaned Gordon. "What do we do now?" I asked, with an air of 'you-got-me-into-it-now-you-get-me-out-of-it.' "Can you afford civvy digs?" "Nope." "Neither can I. Wonder what time the last train is?" "Just gone." I said. "How do you know? I'm going to find out at the next phone box." He went inside the box, and I watched him from the outside, trying to lip-read. After a minute or two, he came out. "Well?" "Just gone" he said.

We walked along in silence, both angry and browned off at this turn of events. "Where are we going?" I asked him, for he solely seemed to have a direction in view. "Police station," he replied resolutely. "Fine," I said, "come out for a night with you and end up in clink." "A Police station isn't clink, haven't you ever slept in a police station before?" he asked, as though it were as natural as the Ritz. "No, I haven't." I exclaimed with dignity. "Have you?" "No." Again we had to ask the way, and we felt a little better when told that it was just around the corner. "Leave the talking to me" said Gordon. "Again!?" I added, acidly.

The Sergeant did not look up as we entered, and we walked to his desk. "Yes, gentlemen?" he asked, as he wrote down things. "Good evening,

Sergeant." Gordon began, with reverence. "You've come to the wrong place for kip," the sergeant said still writing his important document, "Take a tram to the Perth Road Branch. They'll fix you up. More select area. We have too many customers here, and they begin to come in around now. Sorry." He continued writing as he spoke in the clipped Scots accent. And then he looked up. "Word of seven letters meaning 'bend'." He said, thoughtfully. "Refract" answered Gordon. "Thank you, sergeant. Goodnight."

The tram took us to the door of the Perth Road police station; it was nearing midnight and we were both pretty well fed up. The sergeant in charge treated us casually and was evidently used to having Servicemen as guests. "Here's your cell, lads" he said, "you won't find it any comfortable, but at least it's a roof. We'll be making some tea in about ten minutes, and I'll bring you some." We thanked him and looked around the cell. It was absolutely bare, the walls were whitewashed, there was one high window, and near it an un-shaded yellow light. On the bare wooden floor were two piles of blankets. "Those are our beds." I said to Gordon. "I've slept on worse" he said, grinning. "You're a proper adventurous cove, aren't you, Gordon? Does nothing dismay you?" "Nothing at all, old boy." He answered, airily.

The blankets looked dirty and rough so rather than sit on them, I walked around the walls reading the various penciled inscriptions that former occupants had handed down to posterity. I was amazed at the variety of topics discussed. Apart from the more obviously and inevitably crude games, there were pleas of innocence, cries of guilt, articles on higher education, medicine, the law, girlfriends, wives, mistresses, astronomy, sport, politics, even gardening. A long dissertation on why Germany would win the war caught my eye, but as this was dated 1915 I didn't bother reading it. "When you have finished reading the corrugated Gazette," said Gordon, "here comes the tea."

The sergeant brought us pint mugs of tea, and a biscuit. "I'll give you a call at half-six, hope you sleep well." When he went he mercifully left the door open. We sipped the tea, which was hot and good. I passed Gordon a cigarette, and watched him light it. His first mouthful of smoke nearly choked him "I'll kill that bloody soldier." He said. I lit mine. It tasted rubbery, but was not too unpleasant for me to answer, "Oh, I dunno, I've tasted worse."

But Gordon was to have the last laugh. He slept all night in a maddening, comfortable sleep, and I tossed and turned from one side to another. The light was shining, there was a draught from the door, and the blankets were totally inadequate. At one stage I went to ask the Sergeant if I could have another one, but he was fast asleep over his desk, and I didn't have the heart to waken him.

Eventually I was just sinking into unconsciousness when a telephone bell rang, and I was wide awake again. But I had the satisfaction of knowing that the Sergeant had also been wakened. Which indeed he had, for it was the bell of the alarm-clock that had rung, and he came to tell us it was six-thirty. "You look like a dog's dinner" said Gordon, combing his hair. "I feel worse than that," I replied, "If this is a sample of being taken into custody no wonder crime is on the wane." "On the wane? No its not." "Well, it ought to be. It's a disgrace." "Don't preach to me – voice your opinion where every one else does." He pointed to part of the wall. "Write it in that portion, it's appropriate." Across the part of the wall he was pointing at were large black letters which read: - YOU AINT SEEN NOTHING YET, and signed, EX-THE MOOR.

Shivering, we left the cell, thanked the Sergeant as enthusiastically as possible, and stepped out into the empty street. I guessed that the trams would be running, and stood near a stop. "Where are we going?" Gordon asked. "Back to the billet." I replied firmly. "You're mad. We've got all day, yet. What about the ice rink?" "Damn the ice rink, and damn you Gordon, I'm going back to the billet." "Perhaps you're right," he acquiesced, "this place is a bit of a dead loss."

We were both silent until we got into the train. Neither of us had suggested using the wangle, and had bought tickets automatically. As we came into sight of the station I confessed to Gordon, that, with the memory of prison cells close upon me, and in order to clear my conscience, I had bought a return ticket. I opened the window. "I'm throwing this half away." I said. Gordon grinned sheepishly, "Leave the window open." He solemnly tore his ticket in two, and threw away the return half. "Where IS the Christian Science Reading Room?" he asked.

Chapter 3

With the wind whistling through its strutted wings, the Tiger moth was held off for landing. It bounced, took off, landed again, swayed, swerved, bucked, and took off yet again, and then stalled with its nose in the air, resting finally on three points with a dull and heavy thud.

"That," said Flying Officer Burlingford, to me, "was the most diabolical and agonising landing I've ever experienced." I agreed with him. "Taxi over there," he said, waving, "we'll see if you've broken anything." I nearly wept. An undercarriage check was the biggest insult he could have bestowed on me.

We took the aircraft to a small fenced-off area. The fitter looked at me disgustedly as we climbed out, and I stared at the ground as I asked, "Could you check it Corporal. Please?" The Flying Officer undid his parachute straps, and strode off towards the Flight Hut. I followed meekly, like a dog knowing he is about to be whipped, my parachute clanging between my legs like a heavy tail.

When we were out of earshot of the Corporal fitter, F/O Burlingford stopped, and put his 'chute carefully on the ground. He reached for his cigarettes. He needs a haircut, I thought, seeing the hair settling in thick wisps on the back of his collar. He lit up, and I stood by dutifully. The Flight Commander watched. F/O Burlingford blew out a thin line of smoke.

To escape the eager eye of two or three pupils standing only a few yards away, I turned and saw the Corporal gazing intently in our direction. Any time now, I thought. He cleared his throat. I closed my eyes. "Right," he said, "solo. Do a circuit and landing when he's checked it."

I looked at my master, and would have licked his hand. In a dream I signed the Authorisation book and waltzed out to the aircraft. When I was strapped in F/O Burlingford came out to me. "Oh," he said, casually, "don't worry about your landings. I mucked that one up purposely. I wanted to see how you'd correct. Good luck." Lying devil, I thought.

The fitter gave me the thumbs up sign, and I switched on the engine. He swung the propeller, and it sprang to life. Now, no panic, I said to myself. Take it easy. I tested the engine giving the throttle its maximum, and holding the stick back into my stomach. I throttled back, and waved away the chocks. I made for the far boundary for take-off, and bumped along. As soon as my back was turned on the Flight Hut, my morale collapsed. What if the engine stalls on take off? What if I get a puncture? What's the cockpit check again? What if I prang on landing? What made me join the Air Force? I thought of this in about two seconds.

I zigzagged round the boundary, and took up the position for take-off. I tried to remember the checklist for take-off, but I couldn't. It ended in FF.

What was the rest? And then I muttered feverishly TMPFF, and said it over and over again. I tried to concentrate, and all the time the words and tune of a popular song were pounding through my mind. I turned the aircraft cross wind, and did the cockpit check automatically. I searched the sky for aircraft, and saw a solitary Tiger at about two thousand feet. My hands were sweating and I grabbed the stick my too tightly. Then I turned into the wind, chose a tree on the horizon, and opened the throttle slowly and evenly headed for the tree. I pulled the stick back slightly and glanced at the speed. 60 – Dead on, and she was away. At full throttle the aircraft climbed gracefully, now and again gently heaving to one side, and correcting itself in the same instant.

That popular tune that had been in my head all day suddenly burst forth, and I was singing, but could not hear myself. I felt exhilarated; this was living; this was the moment I would never forget, I was in charge of a bucking aeroplane, and I had it in control. At 600 feet I turned gracefully to port, and glanced down at the field. It wasn't there. I looked backwards, and the Tiger Moth started to skid crazily, and immediately threatened to stall. Where the hell was the airfield, I thought. I started turning to the left again, and levelled at 1000 feet. I looked down to the left of the aeroplane at where the field should have been, but it still wasn't there.

I looked down to starboard. No airfield, only a ribbon of a road, and ploughed fields. My palms sweated on the stick. I looked ahead, behind again, left and right, but could see nothing that I recognised. Burlingford will be tearing his hair, I thought. Old Gordon will be laughing his head off, and I shall probably prang. I scoured the sky for other aeroplanes to see in what direction they were going, but the sky was empty. I was alone, and they were all down there laughing at me. I turned to port again, lost height down to 600 feet, and then automatically turned to port again, and there, dead ahead, was the airfield, and my flight path was parallel with the landing tee. Where in God's name have I been, I wondered. I'll probably have to see the Flight Commander for wandering away from the circuit. At the best I shall have to listen to some of Burlingford's profanities.

I landed in one piece, and taxied slowly to the Flight Hut, not very anxious to leave the cockpit. I climbed out, looking hurriedly for my instructor. The fitter walked over to me. "Where are the instructors?" I asked "Having tea. Did you want Burlingford? He said to tell you to sign the book, and get weaving." "No, I didn't want him. Thanks." I said, relieved.

Nobody, not even Gordon, mentioned my solo. They were all too busy discussing leave, which I found out, was fixed up for the next day. I realised I must have scraped in my solo just on the twelve hours. "Coming down town tonight?" Gordon asked. "Last spree, and all that." I asked him if he was meeting Gertrude. "I wish you wouldn't call her Gertrude, it sounds awful. Yes, I am. But I think she'll bring a friend, if I ask her." I had sampled this blind date before, and had been saddled with a land army girl twice my age that sucked extra strong peppermints and said "yep" as though she were a cowboy. "No thanks Gordon, I might just go to the camp cinema."

However, the camp cinema was filled and I was unable to get a ticket, so Gordon tried again. "Come on, I'll phone Gert. She'll fix you up." I agreed. It was my last night anyway, and I had nothing to lose. We met them in the lounge of the best hotel in Perth, had one drink in the bar, but decided to move on when officers started eyeing us.

As it happened Gert's friend, Brenda, was an attractive and amiable sort of person. She didn't talk very much, but was the type who asked intelligent question, and listened intently to the answers. Consequently I was soon shooting horrible lines at her, and she seemed to swallow them. "Tell me more" she would say, after I had painted a shocking picture of a particular Corporal. Service life to her seemed to be something entirely new; something she didn't quite understand existed. "I'd no idea" she would say.

Gordon and Gertrude left us after a while, and I took Brenda to a Café, and enjoyed myself, and enthralled her, by giving a detailed account of life at the Initial Training Wing where I had been for some twenty weeks. I took it week by week, and the story lasted a long time. The size of the bill made me wince when I collected it, but it was worth it, for I had got a lot off my chest. "That was better Spam than we get in the mess." I said to Brenda when we were outside again. "Was it?" she said, "Why, are the meals not too good?"

I was away again, and this lasted until we paused outside a small park. "Care to go for a walk?" I asked. It was still light, so she agreed. I began to regret that this was my last night here, and that I had only just met Brenda, but decided to make the most of it.

I asked her to write to me, and she agreed. "Promise you'll write back?" she said. I promised as though I were making a tryst. There were a lot of people walking through the park, and Brenda suggested we go somewhere quieter. We found a cosy corner in the park, and as we smoked I told Brenda about life in the R.A.F. She was a good listener, and when I told her that I'd been put down for a fighter pilot, she believed me. She squeezed my hand, and I felt like a hero.

Back at camp Gordon was already in bed, and so were most of the other occupants of the hut.
"How did you get on?" he whispered. "Ugh" I grunted. I heard Gordon snigger. "What's the matter? Her 'passion freezers' put you off?" he asked. I scowled in the dark. "How do you mean 'passion freezers'?" I queried. "Didn't you know she was a WAAF?" Gordon asked. My face suddenly felt quite red, and I was glad we were leaving Perth the next day.

Chapter Four

The leave was over, and I was in Manchester. I arrived one Sunday evening, collected bedding from the stores, and was assigned to a hut. There was no-one in, and I set off to the NAAFI. One solitary airman was eating a bun as though it were his last meal. I was pleased to see that it was Ron who had been at Perth. We were acquaintances only, as he had been in a different flight. "You married?" he asked. "No!" I laughed. "You'd be cheesed off if you were."

I was forced to agree, but as the subject didn't interest me I started to talk about something else. Ron fell silent, and I felt a little sorry for him. He had a wistful face, but at the same time boyish, and openly honest. He had a good face, and seemed to be the sort of person it would be nice to have around in an emergency. I began to feel sorry for his wife; she would be missing him. "Have you a picture of your wife?" I asked. He gave me a shocked look. "Oh, I'm not married" he said. "Oh, I gathered that you must be---" I began. Ron shook his head. "No," he continued, "I was only thinking of the poor blokes who are married. They must find it hellish leaving their wives. Especially to go overseas. It's bad enough leaving parents." "Ah, you can't go around carrying other people's troubles on your shoulders." I remonstrated. He shrugged. "I suppose not," he said, but he looked worried, and as though he had a firm intention of carrying everyone's troubles. Then he smiled, "How about going into town for a beer?"

There was no-one else at the camp either Ron or I knew, so we guessed that their leave must have been lengthened. There was little to do there, apart from preparations for going abroad. The camp was a large pool, from which batches of airmen left regularly to go to various destinations overseas. We drew fling and tropical kit, had inoculations and vaccinations, parades and meals. The rest of the time we waited patiently, and spent the evening at The Mousetrap in Manchester. Ron and I were hoping that we should get a posting together, and it seemed quite likely the way things were going. But the weeks dragged on. We went to an orchestral concert, and I heard, for the first time, Beethoven's Fifth Symphony played fully, and beautifully, by the Halle Orchestra. We went to Belle Vue; we went to see Casablanca which was ending a long run at the 'Gaiety'. The song in that film, As Time Goes By, seemed to be a sign of the times for us, it was passing and we were standing still. I began to wonder if I had forgotten how to handle a Tiger Moth, and wondered how long it would take me to solo again.

And then it happened. I was digging a small plot of land in front of the Sergeant's Mess. The Corporal I/C Postings came to me. "Boat." He said. "Get your clearance chit from the S.W.O." I dropped my spade. "Where to,

Corporal?" I asked, holding my breath. "South Africa." He said. I wondered if her were telling the truth.

Ron had not been posted, and as he was the only one of the old crowd I knew in the transit camp, I felt a little sad to say goodbye to him. Although we had only known each other a few days there was an earnestness about him and a quality of brotherhood which I found irresistible, and it was like saying goodbye to someone I had known for years. He gripped my hand and said seriously, "Take care of yourself."

The ship was at Greenock, and I got quite a thrill walking around the deck of an ocean-going liner. It was an American passenger ship which had been converted to a trooper. I could see the barrel of an anti-aircraft gun peeping from a tarpaulin covering at the stern; this appeared to be all the armament she was carrying. Thousands of troops boarded the vessel, and we queued up incessantly for life-belts, emergency rations, and American cigarettes.

I found myself billets on a top bunk of three in a dormitory holding about five hundred men. Near at hand was a wash place, with rows of neat white washbasins round the walls and rows of equally white toilet basins arranged in rows. This bought forth the comment that Henry Ford, with his passion for mass production, must have designed the ship.

A meal was served in the evening. The dining hall was run on a cafeteria system, the whole meal being served on a tray with various compartments, and taken to a table to be eaten standing up. It needed little imagination to see what the meal would look like when we reached the Bay of Biscay.

The ship sailed during the night, so we had not the satisfaction of seeing England disappear from view. We awoke to a grey cold mist and the scream of gulls.

I was on early breakfast, served at 7am, and early supper, served at 5pm. There were just two meals a day, which was apparently all there was time for, for the meals were served continuously throughout the day, as soon as one sitting was finished, another started.

After a few days of this, the weather still being cold, we began to feel decidedly hungry, especially at night. There was little to buy in the canteen, except sardines and condensed milk, although there was no shortage of cigarettes at duty free prices. We began saving bread from the evening meal and making our own snack at night with the sardines, and using the condensed milk as sweet.

In the Bay, although the weather was fairly calm, it was quite an ordeal landing a tray to a table with over-spilling the contents onto the neighbouring compartments. Porridge would get mixed with stew, and pulped fruit, the bread became soaked in milk and sugar, and the whole lot become a messy hash.

One morning, after a heavy sea, the stew and fruit disappeared for breakfast, and we were served with hard boiled eggs, bread and butter, and a large slice of bacon. There was no chance of this spilling, and I went triumphantly to a table and began peeling my eggs. I took a mouthful of this delicious meal, and the man next to me vomited all over his tray. I could have easily thrown him overboard; but I braved it out, and staring at the ceiling got on with my breakfast. But it was too much; the egg was choking me, and, grabbing the second uncracked one I went on deck.

There was a buzz going around that there would be an issue of chocolate from the canteen that day, and I realised with dismay that I was on picket duty that morning. However, by the time I had finished the duty the canteen had not opened, and I joined the end of the queue. The queue stretched round the whole of the deck, a sitting queue at that. Schools of cards were formed; domino enthusiasts were playing it out; anything to pass the time. I opened a book, and before I had read the first chapter a great shout went out – the canteen had opened, and was indeed selling chocolate. The queue did not move for a long time – probably those in front were stretching out a bit, and when it did begin to move the rate of progress was slow. The afternoon wore on, and I began to wonder if it would be my lot to be near the head of it at tea time. But by five o'clock I still had a long way to go, and I was obliged to ask one of the professional queue sitters to sit in for me whilst I went for my meal. This he promised to do for a fee of fifty cigarettes.

I ate my meal quickly, for it was unappetising, and the thought of chocolate had pushed the thought of all other things out of my head. I found my man again, and was pleased to see that he had made considerable progress. I settled down with my book again, and every now and again moved up a few paces, until eventually progress was so fast that it seemed to be useless sitting down between moves.

And then, with only a short journey to go, we heard with dismay the dreaded notes of the ship's bell calling us to lifeboat drill. It seemed too awful to be true, until the confirmation came over the tannoy system, and we had to leave our queue, most of us with thoughts of mutiny. I realised it would be impossible to start queuing again; for my lifeboat station was at the other side of the ship, and I would not stand a chance of getting anywhere near the canteen.

I wandered round the deck after the drill, and saw the queue almost halfway round the ship again. A little later I felt someone tugging at my sleeve. It was a queue sitter. "Here," he said, "You didn't get any did you?" I shook my head. He handed me some bars of chocolate. "Six bars. Yours for half a crown and fifty Gold flake." I asked him how he managed it. "I've been round four times today," he said. "Nothing else to do. I'm not going round again, though; they'll be shut in five minutes." A sudden thought struck him. "Here," he said, "how would you fancy a chicken leg?"

I looked at him as though he were mad. "Follow me," he said.

He led me past sprawled bodies of airmen, soldiers, and marines on to a lower deck, and towards the stern. We went through a companionway, and I knew we were going into the crew's quarters. I also knew this was out of bounds. We went down some more steps, and met a huge Negro coming up.

And then, we were in the crew's galley. An American merchant sailor in a blue shirt and jeans was frying sausages. He grinned when he saw us, and my companion said to him, "Hi, Red." "Hey, Mac," called the American to someone through another companionway, "your goddamned relations are here." "Pete's courting my sister," explained my escort, "I find it very convenient." He turned, and shouted, "Hey, Pete, can I come in?" "Come right in," shouted a voice. We went into a small dining room, quite luxuriously furnished, with small tables, and chairs, and there were even napkins on the table. My friend led the way to a table at which sat a young blonde American.

"Eaten yet?" he asked. I was nodding my head, when the escort said, "No, not yet. By the way, this is Bill, a friend of mine." The American shook hands with me, and I found no cause to tell him that my name wasn't Bill. "Take a seat. Get two cold chickens for my buddies." He shouted to the galley. "Okay, Mac."

We sat eating and talking with the American for some two hours. He was the soul of hospitality, and quickly allayed my fears when I mentioned that I thought it was out of bounds. "You're my guests," he said. "If anyone comes snooping around, leave them to me." But no one disturbed us, and I was sorry when it was time for us to go, as Pete had to go on duty. "I suppose this will cost me a hundred cigarettes?" I said facetiously to my friend. He grinned. "No," he said, "I'll settle for the usual fifty." He held out his hand. I didn't see him again for the whole voyage.

One afternoon, when the ship had reached the tropics, we were on alert, and all the troops were confined inside. We heard the drone of aircraft, and while most of us lay on our bunks reading or talking all hell was let loose. The ship rocked and swayed, and turned and heaved, there were some terrifying explosions, lots of shouting, the pounding of the ship's one gun, and eventually complete silence. We had not been able to see anything of what was going on, for the dormitory was sealed up, and when we eventually did go on deck, there was no sign of anything untoward. We learned later that a large Focke Wulf had been shot down by anti aircraft from another ship in the convoy.

Only once on the voyage were we attacked by submarines. This was in broad daylight, and once again the troops were sealed off. We could hear the thud of depth charges, and then again the silence. As many as possible were accommodated on deck that night, and an abandon ship practise was held in the middle of the night.

The whole convoy reached Freetown with no apparent mishap. Oil tanked was blazing fiercely in the harbour, despite the precaution of the anti submarine boom there, but we heard that there were no casualties.

This short stop at Freetown did much for our morale. The little Negroes diving for pennies, and the banned fruit boats, with the crews endeavouring to seal their wares to jeering Tommies compensated for the long dreary weeks we had spent. We smothered ourselves in anti-mosquito cream, and yearned for the strip of vegetation less than a stone's throw away.

We sailed at night, and spent the rest of the voyage staring down at the phosphorescent sea, or up at the southern hemisphere skies, which at night presented a beautiful sigh. Flying fish skimmed over the lower decks, and one day a school or porpoises frolicked near the ship.

Capetown appeared towards the late afternoon, and two days later we landed at Durban. We had been on the ship for over five weeks.

Chapter 4a

Durban was utopia – lush, warm, gilded and chromed, with the war a million miles away. We tumbled off the ship as soon as she was tied up for a four hour unforgettable spending, eating and drinking spree. I joined up with a sandy haired pupil who had bored me for many long weary hours on the ship talking of far above my head classical music.

"I've a mind," he said, "to see if there's a concert anywhere." "After we've eaten." I was in no mood to see a concert before some decent food; the thought of two ship meals a day was still fresh in my memory. He agreed, and we piled into the first café we came across. It had an Indian proprietor standing at the door, cool and aloof, with Indian waiters hiding behind inscrutable and ingratiating smiles. We ordered a thick steak, with trimmings, and a Castle Lager a piece, and sat back smoking and watching the crowds passing the door. This, I decided, was the life.

The steak arrived, covered with two enormous fried eggs, onions, sausages, bacon, liver, kidney, boiled rice and some curious vegetable that I had never seen. "My shrunken stomach will never accept this!" cried Coop, the sandy-haired lover of music. Nevertheless, we attacked our plates, and demolished the lot, finishing with a delicious banana split which again didn't stop at the banana part; I thought it must have contained everything they had in the kitchens.

We were in the café the best part of two hours, and including the lager we were charged four and six d each, and it was worth every penny. On subsequent occasions I went into that café many times, but was always charged at a comparative exorbitant rate for the same thing – perhaps the proprietor had made a mistake – I certainly hope that we hadn't given them the impression that we were off the ship and starving, although we were.

We strolled round Durban then, watching the magnificent Zulus pulling their rickshaws, plying for fares near the wide white beaches. We marvelled at the modern fast cars that seemed to be everywhere, we listened to the noise of the city – the hum of conversation in a hundred different tongues, intermingled with the hooting and scurrying of the traffic with always the gentle background of the surf rolling in from the sea,

We found the Municipal Hall which had an orchestra, which wasn't playing just then so Coop was a little disappointed, though I was relieved. He promised to visit on a later date, and I prayed that I would not be invited.

Going back to the ship was like going back to prison after being on a short parole, and everywhere there were signs of over-eating and overspending. Strangely enough no one seemed to be drunk, which was surprising, for the ship was 'dry' which had meant the complete cutting of a staple diet for some people for the five weeks we had been aboard.

However, we were in luck. The next day we were shepherded to a camp about half an hour's train journey from Durban. The billets were brick built huts, with only half a wall. There were no beds, just spaces on the floor where one laid a straw palliase and two blankets, but anything in the open was preferable to the cramp and smelly conditions on the ship. The only complaints came from those of us who were on billet picket, ensuring that no one walked off with the straw palliases. We discovered that meals were served in huge dining rooms nearby and there was a cinema where it was easy to get a seat if you got in two hours before the show started. After that you stood, jostled, clung to window sills inside or outside, or if you were wise you went to Durban for a spot of luxury.

Our days were spent sending food parcels by the score, swimming or lazing on the beach, visiting the cinemas, cafes and bars which were in bounds or at the various clubs where hosts of hospitable South Africans queued for the pleasure of showing you their homes and their country in general.

There was no work to do at the camp, which was only a transit camp, and the only time we lifted a finger, apart from the billet pickets, was when we encountered an officer or drew pay. Now and again we studied the posting lists, hoping that the fool's paradise might last a little longer.

Coop got in his visit to the orchestra and, as expected, I went with him. We met two old ladies, who, after the show, hustled us into a car, anxious to hear about where we poor boys came from, and how was dear old Cleethorpes, and had the pier been bombed, and would we like to see the famous monkeys. We had no choice, it seemed, for the car, an open convertible, was soon heading for the open road with a seventy-year-old driver intent on making this the trip of our lives. When one of the ladies wanted to ask a question or to point out something I was horrified to see her turn completely round in her seat, whilst her sister gently took hold of the wheel, and guided the car until her sister was finished. This went on for some miles, with Coop and I sitting in the back whilst the little old ladies shot questions at us, and whooped and laughed themselves along the joyride.

Eventually we reached a road running along the top edge of a small forest. The forest swept down almost to the sea a few miles away in the distance, and we could see Durban spread out to the right, and it almost seemed at our feet. The car pulled up at a vendor, the ladies buying sweets and ice cream, grapes, nuts and oranges. We were not allowed to buy anything, and they bundled their purchases over to us in the back.

Coop and I started into the ice cream, and the car started again, but going extremely slowly so that we might admire the views. Suddenly, and without warning, my ice cream was whipped violently from my hand, and upwards. I heard Coop shout – his had gone too. We looked upward and saw two monkeys grinning down at us, hanging on to the branch of a tree. Both were picking the papers from the ice cream. The two old ladies shook with laughter.

"They always do that! We would have warned you, but we wanted to see the look on your faces." They both went off in a hysterical outburst again as a hairy long arm shot into my lap and made off with a parcel of fruit. "Those monkeys are quick" said Coop profoundly. By now there were dozens of them, jabbering and screeching above our heads, fighting among themselves for the spoils snatched from us.

We kept a weary eye on the branches of the low trees overhead, but the last parcel went sideways, picked cleanly and expertly from Coop's unbelieving hands. "And now you've seen Durban's famous monkeys," said the old lady who was driving; and then, as though she was sorry that the game was over, she announced, "Lets go home."

The drive back was as silent as the night. Conversation was dead, and Coop and I sat back in an embarrassed silence as the little old ladies concentrated on the road.

We arrived back in Durban, and outside the Municipal Hall the car pulled up at the kerb. Without a word, the lady who wasn't driving, turned and open the door. We got out, murmured a thank you, and the car drove off leaving a couple of bewildered airmen wondering what it was all about. Despite that, we set off in search of food, which had been our main pre-occupation before being whisked away by strange old ladies. "Could have been worse," said Coop. "They could have left us there. That would have been a real laugh for them."

Later that night we were on a train back to the transit camp. We sat opposite a South African Corporal who was on the permanent staff at the camp. We told him about the two old ladies. He nodded "We know who those two are, they're harmless enough, just a couple of fading practical jokers." "It's time they faded." Put in Coop, clearly annoyed. "It isn't safe for us boys to be out." "You want to be thankful it wasn't a couple of attractive young women who picked you up!" said the amused Corporal. "I suppose they would have fed us to the monkeys?" I suggested. He shook his head and smiled. "Worse. They'd have taken you home, soused you with drink and good food, there'd be soft lights and sweet music…and then…" "And then…" we both echoed. "Man…" he said, raising his palms outwards, and leaving the rest to our imagination.

"And where do we pick up such awful specimens of South African hospitality? "Certainly not at the Municipal Hall!" cried the Corporal, curling up his nose. "Here, I'll tell you what to do." He took a notebook from his pocket, flicked through a few pages, and then looked up. "Blonde, brunette or redhead?" he asked. I felt as though the devil were in me, so I said redhead. Coop plumped for blonde.

30

"One blonde, one red," said the Corporal, flicking through his pages – "two friends. Here we are." He tore a page out of his book. "That's where to go, and that's where they live, that's their name, and if you don't have a good time my names not Johannes van Ryneveldt." "Oh, is that your name?" I asked innocently. "No," he said, and sensing some domestic South African joke I let it go.

We were grateful to him for the information, and thanked him. "Think nothing of it, man. Glad to help out. One day I might be over in your old country and you can do the same for me." Coop and I studied the names and addresses with high glee. No more orchestras and food parcels for us. High Society here we come.

We said goodbye to the Corporal at the camp gates, and picked our way through the darkened billet lines to our hut. We undressed in the dark, and were getting under our blankets when my neighbour, roused from his slumbers by someone breaking wins said in a sepulchral voice. "You two. Do you know you're posted?" "Which two?" "You two. You and him." "No" I said. "Honest?" "Yes, tomorrow. Parade at HQ. Half past nine. Your going to Pretoria and Coop to Benoni." "Well if that just isn't our luck Coop," I said. "Ah, well," he sighed, "there are probably no monkeys up there!" "Nor nice attractive females either, who lure you to their flat and…" "BELT UP," said the sepulchral voice.

I walked along Johannesburg's main street for the first time. The bustle of yet another great city was intriguing. I marvelled at the near sky-scraper effect of the beautiful buildings, all modern, white and cool. The city, modern as it is, is built in blocks – there is but one diagonal street in the whole city boundary. Consequently it is difficult to get lost.

I nudged my companion. "Just a minute, Coop," I said. A sudden thought had stuck me as we passed a Red Cross recruiting hut in the square. I walked up the hut which had an open window with collecting boxes arranged along the ledge. I tapped gently, and a matronly figure of a lady in a distinctive uniform of the Red Cross appeared. She smiled in a businesslike way.

"Excuse me," I begun, "I wonder if you could help me." The nurse continued smiling. "It its at all possible," she said. I explained that a friend of mine from England was in a hospital near Johannesburg. I had no idea which one, the only information I had was his name and rank. I had written home for the address, but knew that it would take a month to reach me.

"Do you think it would be possible to contact him?" I asked, "And who would be the best people to enquire from?" The nurse considered for a moment, pursing her lips. She put on a pair of glasses, bent her head over a pad and asked me to repeat the name. Briskly she said, "Wait here – give me ten minutes." "What's this all about Jon?" asked Coop.

I explained again to him, and said that I might possibly get some information. Before I could go into too much detail the nurse reappeared. "Well, there you are," she said, handing me a slip of paper. "There is your friend's hospital. It's about 8 miles out. Buses go from just round the corner. If you go now you'll be in time for visiting hours."

It had been as easy as that. I could hardly believe my good fortune, and thanked the lady profusely. She smiled, and looked as though she had been glad to do it. I walked away highly excited, and asked Coop if he would excuse me if I went up there straight away. "Excuse you? I'm coming with you!" He barked.

We found the bus stop, and joined the queue, but it was half an hour before a bus came. I asked the driver if he went past the hospital, but he told me there were no more buses out there that day. It seemed there was no regular service, a private company running special buses on certain days instead. We had, it seemed, just missed one. I felt terribly disappointed, and we were on the point of turning away when a man tapped me on the shoulder. He was a well to do gentleman, and wore rimless glasses and an alpaca jacket. I thought he was an American until he spoke, and then it was a faint welsh accent.

"Excuse me," he said, "but did I hear you say you wanted to go up to the hospital?" I nodded, and told him what happened. He frowned, and then walked over to a lady. They conversed for a few moments, and then he came back. "My wife wonders whether you would care to have tea with us, then we'll run you out there."

I was overwhelmed, and began protesting. His wife came over, a most charming lady, with a persuasive tongue, and again I detected the lilting tones of Wales when she spoke. How I wish that Taffy had been with us. "Now," she said, "slip into that phone box, and phone the hospital. Tell them that you are just out from England, and that you want to meet your friend, but cant possibly go during visiting hours. Ask them if it would be alright if you went up tonight."

I got through to the Orderly Room, and stated my case. After holding the line I was told that, though irregular, I could go that night, providing I did not stay longer than one hour. I was astonished when the military voice asked me would I like my friend to be told or was it a surprise. I did not think such humanity existed in hospitals, especially military ones.

Mr and Mrs. Evans were waiting for me, and from the look on my face they guessed everything was alright. Coop had been amusing them with his reminiscences, and seemed to be getting along like a house on fire.

They took us to tea at the East African Café, where large three bladed fans whirred to the accompaniment of a small orchestra, and the waiters wore tarbushes, and long white gowns with a red sash splashed across the middle. We had tea and pancakes with honey while the Evans's spoke nostalgically of Wales, which they hadn't visited for more than twenty years. Although they had been in South Africa for forty years they still spoke of Cardiff as home, and I was surprised by the way they had kept their accents.

Time flew by, and it was time to go to the hospital. We went to our host's home to enable him to pick the car. They lived in a small villa on the outskirts of the city. Like the rest of the buildings the house was white, and the rooms were large and sumptuously decorated. We went inside for a moment while Mr. Evans got the car out, and soon we were speeding along the road to the hospital.

The hospital was situated in large grounds, and looked like an enormous military camp. Again all the buildings were white, and they were all bungalows. Each ward consisted of a separate bungalow, and when I enquired at the Orderly room a nurse showed me the way to the ward when my friend was lying, whilst the Evans's and Coop remained in the car.

When the nurse left me at the entrance to the ward, she gave me a pass to show to the sister on duty. I entered the ward. It was in complete darkness, and a film was being shown. I picked out the silhouette of the sister who asked me in a whisper what I wanted. I explained as best I could, and she told me to follow her. I walked down the ward following her, still waiting for my eyes to become accustomed to the gloom. Amidst plenty of shushing the sister ushered me to the bedside of my friend.

I stood for a moment looking at him. He had seen me and the looked back at the screen, for of course, in these circumstances, he would not have recognised me. He looked thinner than I remembered, and as I saw him sitting quietly there, his face lit by reflection from the screen, a lump came to my throat, and I longed to turn and leave. But instead I took a step forward and whispered his name. "Who is it?" he asked. I told him, again in a whisper. "Who?" he asked again. I repeated my name, and edged a bit nearer. He took one look at my face, and let out a roar. "No!" he bellowed.

Everyone in the room shushed him, and he started talking quickly in a whisper. I whispered back, and told him why I had come in this manner. I apologised for coming in the middle of the film, but he was excited, and wouldn't listen. He kept on talking in a high-pitched whisper, and then he suddenly lay back on the bed exhausted. I called the sister, and she said I had better go. I whispered that I would be back from a proper visit on the next day, and left the ward.

As I walked back to the Orderly Room I cursed myself for acting so stupidly, and not letting him know that I was going, or at least for being persuaded to go out of visiting hours. I may have done untold damage, I told myself. Didn't I realise he was a sick man? I wished so badly that I had waited.

When I got back to the car Coop asked "Well? Was he surprised?" "Yes, he was. Very surprised."

Chapter 5

It was unbearably hot. Tim and I wandered to the mess for lime juice. The ante room was cool and inviting, but the transformation had taken place. Gaily coloured streamers were hanging from wall to wall, and there was an air of festivity about the place.

"What the hell's that?" said Tim. "A Christmas tree!" I told him. "It's Christmas, remember?" "Christ. A bloody Christmas tree. Who's Santa Claus?" "The C.O." I answered. "Didn't you know? This is one of his little fads. He thinks we might be homesick." "But dammit we're not kids!" said Tim indignantly. "Look at it, lights on it, the lot! What a kindergarten mind he must have. Wait until the Instructors kop a load of this tonight – they'll laugh their bloody heads off!"

Although the tree disgusted Tim the arrangements at the bar did not. An extension of time had been allowed that night, which was Christmas Eve, and the bar had been enlarged. A sheet of paper had been stuck on the bar, asking for volunteers to take their beer from basins as there were not enough glasses available. Both Tim and I immediately put our names down.

"Greedy devil," grinned Tim. "I'm going to drink and drink and drink tonight to take my mind of that ruddy tree. And if the C.O. comes in I'll tell him just what I think."

He asked me if my instructor was coming. I nodded. I had asked him, hoping that he would refuse, but he had accepted. Unfortunately that day my flying had not been up to standard, and the instructor had peevishly suggested that I had tried to write him off. I got the impression that he valued his skin too much. When I told Tim he said, "The trouble with these South Africans is that they've no sense of humour." He was off on his favourite topic again, and went on,

"Today, for instance, I went up with Captain Macleod, and it was my first time doing instrument flying under the hood. He asked me what I'd like to do, when I'd taken over. I said 'bale out!' and laughed like a drain. He said 'I see – well, push the hood back, get out of this spin, and land.' No sense of humour – couldn't see the funny side of it, old boy."

"Mr. Smart-Alec," I laughed. "Is Capt. Macleod coming tonight?" Tim nodded. "Yes, so that makes two of us who are unpopular with our instructors. I shall begin by complaining about the tree. What are you going to complain about?" "The beer." It was typical rancid South African Lager, but beer was beer so I didn't feel like complaining.

Other pupils had drifted into the mess ante room now, and Tim and I sought out Alan Afton, whose father owned a diamond mine (so he claimed), in Kimberley. Alan was gesticulating wildly when we say him, as he described how he recovered from a spin at nought feet. "Thought I'd had it, man," we heard him say, in his curiously attractive clipped accents.

"Just recovered in time." "Good job the deck wasn't another foot higher," Tim put in seriously. Alan put on an innocent look. "Yes, man." "Coming to the party tonight?" He nodded.

I asked him if his instructor was coming. "Yes." "Man" added Tim, hoping to provoke our South African friend. Alan grinned. "I wish he wasn't, the trouble with these Raffie instructors is they're so damned dry." "Plenty of beer – don't worry," said Tim. "You know I don't mean that you bloody fool!" said Alan, as Tim winked at me. "They're so damned dry in their manner. Warped sense of humour." Alan looked very serious, and spread out his hands. "But not you gentlemen. Not yet. You probably will be when you get your wings."
"What did old Colville get you to do today?" Tim asked him.
"Well," answered Alan, "He told me to do a roll off the top. The top of a loop, you know? Well, I did a roll off the top and I thought it was pretty good, man. And when I'd done it, all he said was 'right, Afton, now do a roll off the top." I caught Tim's eye. Alan was looking far too serious. "I think this bloke taking the mickey, Tim" I suggested.
"Man" said Tim.

"Drinks on old Afton tonight for taking the mickey out of the Royal Air Force." I announced solemnly, as we went to dinner. During the dinner, Tim asked Alan what he thought of the monstrosity in the ante room, a question he seemed to ask everyone. "What monstrosity?" queried Alan. "You mean to say you've not noticed anything? Nip out and have a look. Go on, I'll watch your grub." Alan came back with no expression on his face. "It's a tree. I hadn't noticed it. Is it really that bad for you?" "Yes! Put there on orders of the C.O. Don't you think that's childish?" Alan gave a non-committal shrug, and when Tim tried to draw him out, he said simply. "I couldn't care less if there were fifty trees in the mess. I'd soon chop a path to the bar. Pass the tomato jam, please." "You really like this stuff, don't you?" said Tim, clearly repulsed. "Love it, man. Best stuff out here." "You're a bloody savage!" cried Tim, in fits of laughter, and Alan grinned.

When we had finished dinner Alan asked us if we wanted the drink we had claimed. He was told to ask us again when we had some of our buddies with us, as we were going for a wash and a change.

Outside the mess, Tim said "Think I'll take the moke (donkey). It'll teach him the way to the billet, and tonight if we're blindo he'll know the way back." He climbed onto the grey, tired looking donkey, one of the many which roamed round the camp for no particular reason. I declined his offer to get up behind, for the poor animal's legs were already buckling. Tim had a way with animals though, and soon he had the donkey trotting merrily away at a good pace. He was soon lost out of sight, and I walked back to the billet alone.

We had a shower, and changed into long khaki drill trousers and bush jacket, and it was dark when we set off back to the mess. "Hope the moke doesn't stray too far," said Tim. "Clot," I said, "you'll never know which one it is in the dark. Or when you're whacked." "I will, you know," he replied. "I branded him," I remonstrated, but Tim laughed. "I tied one of your hankies to his leg. Now if you want your hankie back, you'll have to help me find it." "I'll get you back one of these…" I said, before Tim raised his hand to make his point. "Don't worry, he's a perfectly clean moke." I was not pleased.

The mess ante room was beginning to fill up when we arrived. Some of the instructors were there, already supplied with glasses of beer, with the native waiters hovering around, and filling them silently after the tiniest sip. Most of the pupils were silent, feeling content to let the instructors do the talking. Our turn will come later, I thought, as we moved over to the bar to collect our basins. Tim and I had a drink together, and we were then joined by Taffy.

"What do you think of the tree, Taff?" asked Tim. I groaned at the mention of the damned tree. "Nice job, isn't it?" said Taff. "But I don't see the point---" "Buy the boy a drink!" cried Tim. "Here, Taff. All the best."

I saw my instructor arrive, so I left them to it. I went over to the door to meet him. He was dressed in full uniform and Sam Browne. I greeted him, and he explained that he could not stay for long – the orderly officer had gone sick, and he had stepped in. I took him over to the bar, and gave him a beer. "Good Lord, what on earth are you drinking from Noble?"

I explained the basins. "Ah yes, South Africa is at war," he said. I was confused, but he carried on. "You know, before I came over here…" "Where are you from, sir? I thought you were South African." "No, I'm from Manchester. I've only been here about a year. I was in Brazil when the war started. Civil pilot. And it took nearly two years for me to get here." He explained that his family were in Capetown, and that very soon he was expecting leave before going 'up north', to the Middle East. That explained the 'value of his skin', I thought. He had already logged more flying hours than I could possibly get if I flew regularly every day for the next ten years. "You must get fed up of flying Tigers?" I asked. "No, I don't get fed up. I only get fed up if a pupil doesn't shape the way I want him to. Then it worries me. You don't know how you've worried me. I've had more sleepless nights worrying about you than any other pupil."

I looked down at the floor. The conversation was taking the turn that I was hoping it wouldn't. "But, you're okay now," he went on. "And I'm not worried any more. You are being moulded, and were far too resistant at first. I think your trouble was overconfidence. You soloed far too early in England." I smiled, remembering the struggles I had had to solo.

"You took nearly twice as long under my guidance, didn't you? But you'll find that your future solos on conversion to bigger aircraft will come all the more easily." I gave him another drink. I had had no idea that he took a pupil so seriously. "I shouldn't be surprised if you turn out to one of my star pupils. Only don't be so bloody reckless."

The conversation turned to a more general theme, and I endeavoured to draw Taffy and Tim into it. I felt strangely elated at the Lieutenants words, for just recently I had thought things were going fairly badly, and had indeed felt a little worried. I plied more beer into him, but then he said that he must go.

"Typical" said Tim, as soon as the Lieutenant had gone. "Star pupil. What a line shoot. I hope old Macleod thinks I'm his little blue eyed beauty." Taffy, who was a rather melancholy soul had been looking on and saying nothing. I could never guess what he was thinking, and I wondered now. "What's your instructor like, Taff?" I asked. He finished drinking his beer before answering, and then he turned scornful eyes to me. "First rate, he is. And dead keen. Ex-ops type. Shot down, he was, when flying a Blenheim in Libya. He's resting now." "Some rest! Stooging a load of pupes over the bundu," said Tim. "Hope I never end up doing that." "Oh, I dunno," went on Taffy, thoughtfully, "it could be a lot worse. You've got to be good, you know, to be an instructor. I wouldn't mind it at all."

"We'll all end up as instructors or staff pilots, and stay over here. There's very few postings from SFTS to Blighty, or the Middle East just now." I put in. "We've a long way to go before we posted anywhere," Taffy moaned. I was clear he wanted so badly to be fighting. Tim agreed. "Wait until we get the Wings exam, boys. If we're not washed out now – we shall be on it." "Ask old Macleod what the exam is like, Tim" I suggested. "He's over there – just come in."

Tim walked over, and brought Capt. Macleod over to the bar. We all greeted him enthusiastically, and respectfully. He was an untidy man, with a shock of unruly fair hair, and a short military-style moustache. He was from German West Africa, and most of his pupils agreed that he was a spy. He was a stickler for discipline in the air, and as we all knew, he would stand no nonsense. He was the Flight commander, and we had all flown with him on solo tests. I had been rather surprised when Tim had spoken earlier of his facetious behaviour that morning. Had it been true, I think it would have been mentioned, for it wasn't the sort of thing that Captain took lightly. He was, however, all smiles, and took the beer that Tim offered him with great charm.

"We were just saying, sir" said Tim, "that we were not looking forward to the Wings Exam at SFTS, even though its still quite a long way off." Macleod grinned broadly. "All you pupils seem to worry about is the Wings Exam. I can't tell you anything about the Exam nowadays. It has been a long time since I took mine, and things change." "I suppose flying ability is taken into account?" I asked. "Of course," he nodded. "Flying ability is logged against you through the course. We do it here, and your records go with you." Tim groaned audibly at hearing this, but in an exaggerated manner. "You might well groan," said the Captain, "I've never seen such a lot of ropey flyers in all my experience. You're the worst course we've had through here." We all looked at him open-mouthed. "Any more beer?" he blandly asked, and Tim gave him another pint. "Do you mean that, sir?" Taffy asked.

Captain Macleod handed round cigarettes, and lit up before answering. "Of course I do. Down to a man you think you know it all. And yet there isn't one amongst you who has the makings of a good pilot. Your straight and level isn't straight and level, your circuits and bumps are positively dangerous, and your aerobatics stink. As for rules of the air, I am surprised that there isn't one amongst you that knows even the elementary laws. You're all ham-handed, club footed clots that should be square-bashing in the army."

He took another swig of his beer, and finished it. We stared at him, speechless. "So I wouldn't worry too much about the Wings Exam, if I were you. A good half of you won't be taking it." He looked round us all, grinned, and said cheerfully. "Well, goodnight, gentlemen. Oh, and a Merry Christmas." "I don't believe it. He has ruined my Christmas!" said Tim. "You didn't ask him about the tree?" I said, acting nonchalant. "Bugger the tree. Where's my basin?"

An hour later I'd had enough. The heat of the room, the noise, and the tobacco haze, to say nothing of drinking beer from a large pudding basin was making my head reel. "Let's find the moke." I suggested to Tim.

The animal was not outside where we hoped. We walked between a line of billets calling for him. I found a stick and poked at dubious shadows. Then we spied him standing quietly at the far end of a row of billets near the Corporal's mess. We made a beeline for him, but before we could reach him a Corporal stepped from the shadow's, and pulled us to a halt. "Where are you men going?" "For the donkey, Corporal" we said. "What do you want, or even need, a donkey for?" "To ride home on, Corporal." "He belongs to the Corporals mess. You can't have him." "But Corporal" said Tim, "he's got his handkerchief." We all walked up to the donkey to examine him, and there, sure enough, was my handkerchief tied round the animal's leg. "That's different" said the Corporal. "You'd better get aboard."

He helped us mount, gave the donkey a hefty whack on its rear, which set him off at a good pace. Half an hour later, after a more circular tour of the camp, we reached our billet. I felt quite worn out, and tumbled into bed quickly, glad that every night wasn't Christmas Eve.

We both missed breakfast the next morning, and at about 10 o'clock Alan bounced into the billet, and woke us up. "Heard the latest?" he asked, knowing full well that we were too hung-over to move. "How could we?" said Tim. "We're all confined to camp for fourteen days." "What for?" I was annoyed, as I had made some plans. Alan rolled his tongue around his next words. "Somebody pissed on the Christmas tree."

Chapter 6

I walked into the crew room to sign the Authorisation book. By the side of my name I saw entered 'Altitude Test. Solo.' I felt very pleased with myself. It was a beautiful day with no haze, the very day for a nice quiet stooge about the sky for an hour and a half.

I strapped myself into the Tiger Moth, and the mechanic started up the engine. I had not flown this particular aircraft before, and hoped that she had plenty of power, and was not one of those nearing the end of her journey, worn out by overwork and mishandling.

As I revved her up and tested the magnetos the engine seemed sweet and strong, and I taxied to the boundary with high hopes of reaching a good altitude. The object was to climb as high as possible, log the height, and do aerobatics on the way down to lose height.

I took off and climbed steadily, joining the circuit, and then circling the aerodrome. At about five thousand feet I edged away from the airfield, still continuing to climb, doing gentle turns. I tried one or two steep turns, when the horizons slips onto one side, and the tilted, ever-changing panorama as the turn is continued affords one of the greatest static thrills of flying; but these turns slowed up my progress, and I gave her less rudder and stick easing the turns until they were the gently sweeping type.

It was becoming distinctly colder, and I wished that I had put on more clothes. I saw the airfield below, and could pick out one or two aeroplanes in the circuit. They looked small, and seemed to be travelling slowly. About a mile away I saw the yellow shape of another aircraft at about my height practising loops and rolling off the top. I watched him lazily for a while, flying slowly towards him, until I was well above him and he was lost from sight.

The Tiger was still climbing well, 8,000 feet now, the height I had expected to reach, but there still seemed to be some reserve power, and now and again I would be caught momentarily in a thermal, a strong upward gush of air, and this would help the height, the altimeter spinning once round like a mad thing after a short time lag.

9,000 feet and the aircraft was losing power a bit. I increased the throttle setting, and made the climb shallower. The climb was slow and at times appeared to have stopped altogether, and then the altimeter needle would flicker and move round a little. A few more feet had been gained.

The air at that height was thin, and the aerodrome was at 6,000 feet above sea level, which meant that if I could reach 10,000 feet I should be 16,000 feet above sea level. Not bad for a Tiger Moth in any climate. I felt like getting out to push the aircraft, as now and again she juddered, her propellers threshing at the low pressure air. Slowly the needle came up to the 9,500 mark, and it seemed that this was the absolute limit. The controls were very sloppy, and I had to hold the stick well over, and kick the rudder over to maximum to make any turn at all. I kept a wary eye on the speed, for I knew that I was only just above stalling speed, and if she did stall, many precious feet would have been wasted, as recovery at that height in a low powered aircraft is difficult.

Gradually – very gradually – the needle moved towards the 10,000 feet mark. I sat perfectly still, flying straight, very slowly, and making little progress, and then it was there. 10,000 feet and the Tiger was still flying. I felt exhilarated. What a line shoot to tell the boys, for although this is no great height in wartime flying, it certainly is an extremely good height for this aircraft, which was at least fifteen years old.

I felt very cold, and the thin atmosphere was making my head ache a little, so as soon as the needle flickered on the mark I had aimed at I cut the throttle and power glided gently. Going down was much easier that going up, and for four thousand feet, I trimmed the aircraft and it flew itself.

As six thousand feet, I put the nose down violently. I had been sitting still for too long and wanted some action. The aircraft dived and when the speed was well up, and the nose was well below the horizon, I pulled back on the stick. The nose came up gradually, passed the horizon, and swept the sky in a loop. When I completely inverted I could see the horizon again, upside down. I pulled the stick further back still, cut the throttle, and the nose dropped, as I went into a perfect dive from the loop.

That was the only aerobatic I could do to my satisfaction, as it was the easiest of them all. I seemed to be losing height too slowly, so I decided to try a few more. A slow roll followed by a barrel roll, I did spins and stall turns, and one or two curious cavorting of my own that I should not have done had the instructor been with me.

Suddenly the engine cut out dead. I was at about two thousand feet by now, and quickly dropped the nose, dived, and put into operation the recognised drill for re-starting an engine in flight. But there was not a flicker from it, and I guessed that there must be an airlock in the petrol system. I dived again, tried to start the engine again, but it was no good, it had packed in completely it seemed.

I looked round frantically for the airfield. I could see it, but had no hope of reaching it, for I was now down to a thousand feet. I put it into a shallow glide, and shouted curses at the engine. I tried side-slipping it into action, in fact everything that normally does the trick when one had plenty of height and is just practising. But the only sound was the whistling of wind through the struts.

I realised that there was no point in doing anything now but landing, and I scoured the ground for a suitable field. I found one, and flew in a circuit around it, examining it as best I could for any boulders or ant heaps that might mar the landing, but it looked flat, and I congratulated myself on being so lucky, and so near to a reasonably good landing strip.

I had a rough idea of the wind direction, and did my final approach into this with plenty of height to spare. I had in fact too much height, and at the last minute had to side-slip violently to get into the field at all. As I skimmed along the field holding the aircraft before it touched down, I could see that the surface was by no means as even as I had anticipated. There was a series of small humps, and quite a lot of dark brown stones lying about which I had not seen from the air.

As the aircraft lost flying speed and sunk to the ground in a gentle stall, I felt the landing was going to be good, but then I felt a lurch behind me. There was a distinct scraping noise, and the nose swung violently over, and I felt one of the wings dipping. I kicked on correcting rudder, and the nose swung back, and then over again, and I continued this zigzagging until it crunched to a stop. I breathed a sigh of relief, the wing tips had not touched the ground, and neither had the nose gone up. I undid my straps, switched off, and got out. I felt stiff, and was glad to stretch my legs. The silence seemed very oppressive after the noise of the last hour or so. I bent down near the tail of the aircraft and examined it.

The tail skid had evidently hit something, and been wrenched off completely, the back of the fuselage had taken the force of the slithering and landing, and I realised that it was probably the wrenching away of the skid that had caused the zigzagging.

I turned over in my mind the best thing to do, but first I wandered a little way from the aeroplane and lit a cigarette. I knew that before long someone would appear, and I didn't want to wander off to report my dilemma until I found someone that I could trust to guard it. The field seemed to be miles from anywhere. I listened for the hum of any traffic, but could hear nothing. I didn't expect any, fir I had not seen a road as I came in to land.

After about half an hour I saw some figures coming towards me. They were natives, and they were laughing and joking amongst themselves as they came nearer.

Soon they were at the side of the aeroplane, examining it in detail, and ignoring my presence. They squatted on their haunches, pointing at the undercarriage, at the propeller, and engine and a few of the bolder ones stroked the fuselage caressingly. Finally one of them, a large, ragged individual with a perpetual grin came over to me. He saluted, and then pointed at the Tiger Moth. "Him broke."

I nodded and asked him where there was a telephone. He grinned. "You mend?"

"No," I said, and asked again for a telephone.

"No telephone," he replied.

I asked him how far the airfield was from here. He considered for a few minutes puckering up his face in an intense effort at concentration. Then he beamed, scratched his head, and said, "a thousand miles. Over there." He flung his arms wildly in any and every direction. "What's your name?" I asked him. "Motor car." He answered, without a flicker of an eyelid. "Do you know anybody at the airfield?" I asked.

His grin widened and his large white teeth seemed to fill his whole mouth. "I build him." He looked at the ground and prolonged his inane grin. I could see that it was pointless trying to get anywhere with him, and looked round at the other visitors. They had lost interest in the aeroplane, and were sitting in a group watching me, and I suppose wondering what I was going to do. So was I.

"Anyone know where there is a telephone?" I shouted. They broke out talking and laughing. Motor Car said "No telephone. No understand. No telephone." He shrugged his shoulders, and turned away as though the matter had been dealt with. I called him back.

"Now look here chap," I said, in my most official voice, "I'm leaving you and your friends in charge of that aeroplane. I shall contact someone at the airfield and they will send out a lorry and some men to mend it. You must not let anyone touch it. Do you understand? No-one must touch it." I then proceeded to tell them of all the horrible things the officers would do if that aeroplane was damaged.

I did not mean to go far, for the aircraft was my responsibility and I did not trust these characters. Motor Car rolled his eyes in a pained manner. "I take good care of him. You take me for ride." "You take good care or you'll go for a long ride." I threatened, but I could tell by the way he grinned that once I was out of sight he'd be in that cockpit.

I walked across the scrubland, meaning to have a look at the countryside to see if there was a road nearby. I had looked at the map I was carrying, and seen that I was along way from the main road, but there might just be a chance that there was a track nearby. As I walked I kept turning to keep a wary eye on the aircraft, but the group were sitting quietly in the shade that it afforded. I walked on to a small hillock, and searched the countryside for signs of life. Apart from one or two decrepit looking huts about half a mile away there was nothing. I looked in the direction of the airfield and could clearly see aircraft landing and taking off. By air distance I could not be far from the camp, and I began to wonder if anyone had seen me go down. I walked back to the aeroplane. Some of the natives had fallen asleep under the wings, the rest were just sitting. Motor Car was watching me with interest, but I detected a certain disappointment in his face as he saw me return.

"You find lorry?" he said. I shook my head. "You know I didn't." "I have bicycle. At house. You pay me; I go to airfield and tell." "You go to the airfield first!" I said. He shook his head and laughed, and I began persuading him. When he saw it was useless arguing about money he did eventually say he would go, and soon the whole tribe of them shuffled off led by Motor Car who alternately grinned, shook his head, and looked at the ground.

I prepared myself for a long wait, and was surprised when, after a few moments, I heard the sound of a car. Then I saw the gharry approaching, bumping and swaying over the uneven terrain.

In the front seat was a native driver and my instructor, and there was a group of mechanics in the back. "Been low flying?" the instructor asked, eyeing the smashed tail.

I told him indignantly that I had reached 10,000 feet, and that the engine had cut on my way back down to 2,000. "Iced up, I suppose" he said sarcastically. I felt pretty depressed, and sensed that the instructor thought I'd been fooling around at a low altitude.

I asked the native driver if he knew Motor Car. He was a smart man, in the coloured Corps of the Army. He did know Motor Car, and said that he had worked at the camp, and been dismissed for stealing. "He'd steal anything man."

"Where's the stick?" bellowed my instructor, making me jump slightly. I didn't understand for a minute, until he repeated. "The joystick isn't there. Where is it?" I looked at the native driver. "He'd steal anything!" he laughed.

My instructor laughed it off. "Lucky it wasn't anything else, that's about the only thing that's movable. It'll make him a nice knobkerrie. " I felt that I would like to use the knobkerrie on Motor Car.

Chapter 7

I went with Tim from the lecture rooms to our billet. We had just two hours before night flying. "Christ I'm tired," said Tim, throwing himself onto his bed. "It's all this hard work you're doing," I suggested. "I'm not tired because I'm no fool. I'm going to write a letter." I fiddled in the drawer of the communal dressing table for some paper. "You write too many letters. Who's it to this time? Girl?"
"Mind your chuffing business." I replied. "You'll never get anywhere writing," he continued. "Didn't you know you shouldn't put anything in writing to a woman?" "Got to keep up the old morale somehow," I smiled.

Tim snorted. "A Coca Cola would do you far more good. As I see it, they're a waste of time." He looked across to me, to see if I was still listening. I was, but not intently, for having listened to Tim's misogynistic observations for many weeks now I could guess what was coming. I usually put up some sort of an argument in order to save his the embarrassment of arguing with himself. "A sheer waste of time," he went on. "Take old Phillips. He'd been looking forward to mail from his popsy ever since leaving Blighty and then when he got a letter, what did she say? Sorry, but I've met someone else, and its all over." "That happens all the time, that's why its called a 'Dear John' letter." I said. "He didn't."

Tim was quite right. Glen Phillips was a little older than most of us. He was a small, wrinkled type, his brow for ever furrowed by a frown. He never had a lot to say, but what he did say made sense, and he commanded the respect of most of us because he was a ground staff fitter, a sergeant, and a good one at that. He had been told many times that he was a fool to re-muster when he could have got a good job, probably on an airfield in England, but at the same time he was enormously, though quietly, admired.

When he received the letter that Tim had just mentioned he was in the mess, and had sat down with a few letters. The fatal one he happened to open last. He said nothing at the time, but just walked out of the mess. He didn't turn up for flying duty that afternoon, nor was he in his billet at night, and the next day, after lectures, it was decided that he would have to be found and service police were given the job.

Two days later he just walked back into camp as though nothing had happened, and appeared in the mess at lunchtime. We all gathered round him, but he wouldn't tell us anything at all, and we didn't even then know about the letter he had received.

He was put on a charge, and eventually stripped down to aircraftsman. That didn't worry him at all, and it was only after much badgering that we eventually got word of the letter from him. He wouldn't tell us where he had spent his time out of the camp, though, but these things get around, and we had all been faintly nauseated to hear that he had spent the whole time with a coloured woman. Hence the rather stiff sentence he got.

"He'll never be the same again." Tim said. "I suppose not, but it isn't everybody that goes off the deep end like that, Tim." "Wouldn't you?" "Course not," I replied. "Not to that extent. Would you?" "Wouldn't get the chance old boy. Never have anything to do with them at all. There's far too much emotion in women. I couldn't cope with tears and that sort of thing. I don't even love 'em and leave 'em, I just leave 'em."

He looked at me to see how I would react to his uncouth words. I smiled rather smugly. "For someone who just leaves them, you pretend to know an awful lot about them." "I learn it all," said Tim "from watching the reaction of blokes like you. The little human tragedies that one hears about from time to time are invariably caused by women. You haven't had yours yet, but you will."

I laughed outright, and told him not to talk crap. "You'll get your brush-off letter, you know. The only way you can avoid it is to drop yourself right in the creek like old Les Forester, and get married. And look at him, if there was ever a case for the psychiatrist, its him." "So it's my turn now, is it?" I replied.

"Have you seen him tearing his hair when there's no mail from her? Have you seen him devour his letters like an avaricious wolf? He'll read it time and time again, and then start writing back. Backwards and forwards they pelt each other with these aphrodisiac offerings, and then expect their marriage to last. Not a hope in hell. One day he'll get a letter saying that she's going out with a Naval officer, and then old Forester will turn himself grey trying to read between the lines, and he'll wait with patient horror for the letter saying that she's missed that month, and what---" I broke in. "You vulgar blackguard." "You'll see Noble, if you stick with Forester, you'll see."

I carried on with my letter when Tim had exhausted himself for the moment, for I wanted to get it finished before we went night flying, and it was almost time for the evening meal.

It was dark by the time we went up to the mess, Tim astride his dependable donkey. We looked for mail in the anteroom pigeon-holes, but there was none for either of us. A new course had arrived that day, and there was a whole series of new faces. Alan Afton was holding court with a group of them who watched him with their mouths open as he explained some awe inspiring and probably untrue exploit. When he saw us he grinned and spoke in a lower voice.

He joined us in the mess. "What a shower the new course is," he said as we all sat down. "Half of them can neither read or write. I told them to get their knees brown. Especially the Rafs!" "Good old Alan," said Tim, "make yourself popular as quickly as you can, eh? Did you tell them your dad owns a diamond mine?" "He doesn't, man" said Alan, good humouredly, "only three-quarters of it. The rest is mine."

Tim, who was sitting facing the door, suddenly nodded towards it, and muttered under his breath, "Hell, here comes the bridegroom. Shift up and make it look as though there is no room."

It was too late, however, and Les Forester came and sat down next to Tim, and facing me. He looked in high spirits. "I've just walked up from the camp post office with a new bod," he said, "one of the new course. The post office had sent for him, and gave him two bundles of letters, about a hundred altogether."

"All his?" I asked incredulously. Les nodded. "He was terribly embarrassed. It appears that his girl had promised to write every day, after seeing him off, and she'd stuck to her promise."

"A good pal for you" muttered Tim. "He'd missed his posting from Manchester, and he hasn't written to her at all, and now all this lot has turned up. Is his face red?" "Wait till he starts reading them," I said, "it'll be redder still." "The officer in the P.O. told him to tell the sender to lay off a bit. They had been written in mauve ink, and have given the authorities more than a headache. And the funny thing is he says he only took her out once!"

"Huh, the lying sod," said Tim, "She's not going to let him get away."

Our soup came, and as I broke some bread I watched Les open his letter. This was inevitable. Wherever Les went, there would be a letter, and to be in his company when he was either reading one or writing one was a little wearing.

I bent to my soup, but looked up quickly, when I heard a loud cry of 'oh my god!' from Les. His face had gone pale, and his eyes seemed to be popping out from his head. I noticed that the envelope had fallen in his soup. "What's up, man?" said Alan. "My wife…" said Les, in a bewildered voice. "She's joined the bloody Wren's!"

I looked at Tim, who was almost choking on his soup. "See what I mean? Beginning of the end, Noble. Your head will roll next." Tim pointed at me with his long bony finger.

But Tim, self styled prophet though he was, was wrong in that forecast. Many more heads rolled in the dust before mine eventually did.

Taffy poked his head round the door of the billet. "Are you coming for a last look at Pretoria?" he asked. "There's just time to make the bus." As we were due for posting shortly I thought it would be a good idea. "Yes," I answered, "I must get an SFTS flash for my cap. Perhaps we can see a film?" We could find no other volunteers, but I had a wallet full of orders for new flashes by the time we set off.

The hot and dusty bus had a puncture on the way, and we were consequently help up for a couple of hours. The bus had no spare tyre – we were miles from anywhere, and had to wait until the return bus came from the opposite direction – then we borrowed his spare.

When we finally arrived, I dashed to the shop for the new blue and white cap flashes; they looked neat and important lying in their tissue, and I bought nearly two dozen. "Anything else?" asked Taffy, who was impatient to get the boring job of shopping over with. There was nothing else to shop for, so we went into a bio-café for tea. It was against my better judgement, for the last time I had been to one of these I had a cup of hot tea poured down my neck as the boy and girl went into a fade-out clinch, and I had to miss the cartoon which followed.

However, all went well – we chose a seat where the person behind was not eating – just watching, and I coped with a plate of bacon and eggs quite well. There was no fade-out clinch; it was a Western and ended with the villain lying in the dust with his toes turned up.

The tea with the meal was foul, and I suggested that we nipped out to a milk bar for some more. It wasn't a crowded bar when we found it, and we sat with a cigarette chatting about our next move to SFTS. Suddenly I noticed a girl sitting few tables away. She was watching us, and seemed to be smiling. I nudged Taffy, and tactlessly he swung around. Her smile froze. So it had been meant for me…"You're welcome," he said, and I couldn't understand the note of sarcasm in his voice – she was pretty – a sort of wispy blonde with fine chiselled features. Her blue eyes were pleasant enough, and they gazed rather solemnly at me which gave me quite a kick – there is no man alive who doesn't like being made eyes at – apart from Taffy, so I put his rather cryptic remark down to the green eyed bug.

"Pity she hasn't a friend for you, Taff," I said, magnanimously. But, as it turned out, she did have, and Taffy fell for her right away despite the fact that she was not nearly so attractive.

We made the usual shuffling, giggling and smirking which precede the final "Are you doing anything tonight" type of date, and before long Taffy was paying for four milkshakes, which was quite impressive on airman's pay with an allotment of a shilling a week already docked for his mother's allowance.

Before we dare suggest a walk I realised that another round of milkshakes would have to be bought and quaffed, while the mutual stories of each other's lives were unfolded. Four shillings down the drain in one fell swoop! Ah, well, I told myself, it was worth it – they were nice girls. Or were they?

Our eventual walk took us through the quiet streets of Pretoria which are beautiful at any time of the year. A few yards from the city centre is a green ornamental lake. A fountain plays on the huge ivory lilies nestling on the plate-like leaves, and there are one or two seats arranged round this lake. It's a wonderful place to be with a girl. Taffy and his friend Jean sat on one form, and Pauline, the blonde, sat with me on the next seat.

Quite suddenly my side cap was flung from my head, and at the same moment I heard Taffy shout – his had gone, too. I whipped round. A small crowd of young men were standing silently near us. "Take no notice," hissed Pauline. "Turn around, and go on talking."

Puzzled, I did so, and looked to see what Taffy was doing. He was dusting his cap, and then put it back on his head. I did the same, only to have it whisked off the same instant.

"Say nothing," said Pauline. I said nothing, just picked up my hat, and held it. "What's the trouble?" I asked from the corner of my mouth, the way Cagney would have done in a similar position. She didn't answer, and I had that awful prickly feeling on the back of my neck that one gets when expecting that something unknown but vicious was about to happen.

This time it was my hat that went flying – it was me. A particularly violent push by what seemed to be a dozen arms catapulted me from my seat. Immediately a burst of jeering, mocking laughter came from the two crowds – one watching Taffy, and the other watching me. From the ground I watched them advance and slowly form a circle round us. "Don't fight, whatever you do, don't fight," screamed Pauline, "and don't try to make a break for it."

I had no intention of doing either, and neither did I try to get up – I just sat there waiting for the next move. One of the mob came nearer to me, aimed a kick, and spat. "Raffies!" he said. That did it; the kick I didn't mind, but the spitting I did. I was up on my feet in a flash, and whirled into him like a madman. Pauline shouted "No, don't fight them!" as she started to scream in Afrikaans at them. I still flailed my arms, but didn't stand a chance. The circle narrowed, I was literally pounced on, and held so that not a limb could move – indeed I could scarcely breathe.

I could hear Pauline's plea in Afrikaans, so I couldn't understand a word she said. I tried to turn my head so that I could see how Taffy was faring. I couldn't move an inch. "You alright Taff?" I shouted, as loudly as my compressed lungs would allow, and got a swift smack on the side of my face for the trouble. However, I did hear Taffy's reassuring voice, although his words were cut off quickly and I guessed he was having the same treatment.

Then, as suddenly as the attack had started, it was over, and the hooligans simply disappeared as quickly and as silently as they had appeared. "Well, I wonder what all that was in aid of," remarked Taffy as he dusted himself off. I stretched myself wearily feeling for broken bones, and finding none got on to my feet again. The girls ran to us, and asked if we were alright. Neither Taffy nor I had suffered any damage, though we both looked and felt terribly dusty, and a little war-stained. "You'd better come along to my place," said Pauline, "and get cleaned up." "We're alright, thanks," said Taffy, who clearly wanted to be out of this place, "We'd better be getting back."

I withered him with a look. "Thanks, I could certainly do with a wash," and I saw Taffy shrug resignedly. I couldn't understand his attitude, for the invitation had included him, and of course, his girl friend. As we walked along we gave our interpretation of why we had been so ignobly ambushed and attacked. We still were not clear about it, nor were we clear about the reason for their sudden flight, though I think it had something to do with Pauline and her Afrikaans.

When we reached Pauline's house, I asked: "Are you alone?" "Quite alone, come on in." The house was in a small terrace, and she took us into the front room – it was a little drab, and seemed unlived in. Taffy shuffled in the doorway and his girl gave him a push. "Sit down," she said, indicating at the settee. He sat down, and immediately she was at his side, engaging him in a long and volatile kiss. "Poor Taff," I murmured, "Attacked twice in one night," and patiently waited for my turn. It came. As soon as the light went out, I was pushed onto an easy chair, and gently caressed.

"Co-operate," snarled Pauline as she bit my ear. Begging her pardon for forgetting my manners I co-operated, or perhaps I should say began to co-operate, when I suddenly froze at a sound that could not have been more blood-curdling had it come from a banshee.

 The sound was that of a child, and it said "Mummy". Pauline thrust me away, and said, "Coming, Darling." She left the light off, and went into the next room, and I heard the sound of a child using the potty. The shuffling and murmuring from Taffy's corner had also stopped, and Taffy announced "We'll just make the last bus. Let's go."

I groped round the wall for the outer door, and told Taff to get a shift on. He was there before me, however, and we opened the door into a little hall, and from there let ourselves out into the street.

We fled down the street, Taffy keeping a commentary on the likes of people like me who must have been born blind or daft or both.

"How was I supposed to know she was married?" I panted. "What do you think she had a wedding ring on for?" I hadn't noticed the ring, and even had I done I would not have expected a seduction scene. I explained that to Taffy, and he got madder.

Suddenly I stopped running. "Taff, I'll have to go back." "You go by all means noble; I'll inform your next of kin." "I mean it Taff. I've left something." "Hell, what," said Taffy, fearing I think that it may have been something that would incriminate him. "Two blasted dozen white and blue cap flashes, that's what!" The sound of Taffy's cackle of laughter rent the air like a thunderclap. Eventually he said, quite calmly, "I wonder what she'll do with them if her husband isn't aircrew?"

Chapter 8

Before the train puller out of Pretoria station the card fiends were traversing the corridors looking for recruits. I declined when I heard that the game would be poker. "Call me when you play pontoon." I remarked.

We were four to a compartment, which was extremely comfortable, and we had nothing to do but sit and enjoy the scenery. As we all had been working at high pressure doing the final exams during the last few days the complete relaxation for some hours that the train journey was going to afford us was welcomed by everyone.

The train chugged steadily away from Pretoria, and soon we were in wild country. It was early morning, and was not hot yet, but already in the distance we could see a haze rising steadily heralding the heat of another hot summer day. We were travelling north, towards the equator, and were going down gradually, from an altitude of 6,000 feet, to which we had grown accustomed to.

I stared out of the window lazily contemplating this new move. I felt excited, as one usually is when going on a journey, and I wondered what the other end had in store. This was the last journey before we got our wings, and although there was some twenty weeks to do I had a feeling that at long last the coveted wings and qualification was really in sight. It's a long upward climb, a disgruntled sergeant had once said, "and I wouldn't do it again for all the nuts in Brazil."

It had been a long upward climb. From the first week as a recruit when I smoked my first cigarette, and drank my first tankard of beer and tried desperately hard to keep my hat flash white, and my buttons clean, then to the few weeks 'toughening up' under canvas when I made breeze blocks for camp buildings and dug ditches for the sewage. Then through the long gruelling six months at the Initial Training Wing where the nearest aircraft were visitors strafing the sea front, and we crammed the Morse code, navigation, armament, flight theory and meteorology into embryonic service brains, sluggish with nights on fire and gas picket.

Leaves which went all too quickly, and then a posting to a flying school for some twelve hours instruction, more leave, a transit camp, the ship, a lazy week in Durban – paradise after austere London or Manchester.

My thoughts meandered on – E.F.T.S. which we had just finished. It was mostly lectures and flying, with an occasional trip to Pretoria or Johannesburg. And now the train again – another move, this time after four or five months some of us would get our wings. "Me, neither," said Tim, who had sat still and quiet for too long. I saw he had in his hand an enormous chocolate bar; it must have weighed a pound.

"I'll put it in my sun hat, and then no bounder will snaffle it." He undid the tapes of the bag covering his sun helmet, slid the chocolate inside, and placed it on the rack. "I'm glad to see the back of that place," said Tim. "Never though I'd make it through S.F.T.S." "You're too modest," said Geoff Barker, the third occupant of the train compartment. "The thing that surprised me about you is that you didn't go on singles. I always thought you were batchy enough for singles."

This was a sore point for Tim. He had badly wanted to do his further training on single-engine aircraft, and eventually pass on to Spitfires or Hurricanes. Although he said very little about his enthusiasm for flying I had gathered over the last few weeks that he was dead keen, and he had been dreadfully disappointed when told of his posting to twin-engine training. He now fostered the hope that he would, later on, be able to pull a few strings, and get on twin engine fighters. It was a vague hope, for having trained on twins, if he did manage to reach an operational squadron he would no doubt go on bombers. "I'm surprised you ever got past the selection board!" Tim said cuttingly. "They must have been hard-up when you joined."

Barker whistled slowly through his teeth, and smiled at Tim in a patronising manner. He was probably considering his last remark, for they had both joined at the same time. Alan Afton stirred in his seat, where a moment before he had been snoring. "Shut up, please, gentlemen." Tim pushed him good-humouredly. "Aw, get back to your Swede bashing." Alan opened one bleary eye, looked disdainfully at Tim, and closed it again. "And to think," said Tim, "that a few weeks from now, we shall probably have to call him 'sir'. There's no justice." Alan mumbled his stock reply to most questions, "You shouldn't have joined, man." And then he was snoring again.

The compartment door opened, and the little wrinkled face of Glen Phillips eyed us. "Anyone for cards?" "What are you playing?" I asked him. "Poker."

"Give me a call when it's Pontoon" I said. "That's his game, Pontoon. No good at anything else," said Tim. Geoff Barker turned to Phillips and said, "Don't you know it's illegal to gamble on trains?" Glen's face wrinkled into a smile. "Even when you're winning?" he asked innocently.

"You might be winning now but if you're caught, you'll lose it all!" "Well I'm not winning; I'm trying to find someone that I can beat." "I wouldn't gamble a ha'penny of my money on a train or anywhere," Barker went on.

Tim winked at me. How well we knew it. Barker was a Yorkshire-man through and through, and very tight with his purse strings. He always drank lemonade in the mess, would stand in on a free round, but would never buy one. He also ran a money lending business – lending small amounts to trustworthy pupils, and charging an exorbitant interest. He had become very distracted when a pupil who owed Barker thirty odd shillings in loans and accumulated interest had been posted to another school, and had in effect told him that he could whistle for his money.

Phillips ignored Barker. "I'll give you a yell when the Pontoon starts," and with that, he left us be.

The train began to slow down and it approached a small station. There was no platform, just a collection of huts. I let down the window, and when the train stopped, with a lurch, I watched the porters unload a few bags of mail. A large group of small native children scurried along the track holding their hand out, their months opened in their wide, characteristic grin. Some of them could have been no more than two years old, and were completely naked, their little pot-bellies banging on their thighs as they bounded along.

Arms reached down from the train giving them sweets, chocolate and cigarettes. One little urchin who looked about two grabbed a cigarette from a large and tough-looking lad, and stuffed it into his hat with an air of 'I'll have that later.' All the time they grinned, whooped, and shouted obscenities, the choicest coming from the youngest members of the tribe.

"Wherever have they picked up such awful language?" said Barker in a shocked voice, suggestive of a Methodist minister. "Only one source," said Tim, "from trains passing through. So shut up."

The leader of the gang came near our carriage. He looked up at us and grinned. "You gif me fife Woodbines," he said, "I bring my sister. She do striptease." He laughed, and grimaced.

"If I give you ten players, what will she do?" Tim asked laughingly, but we didn't want to hear the boy's reply, and the train had started moving again anyway. The country became even sparser in its vegetation and population, and for many miles neither a house nor person was seen. It was a scene of wild shrub, flat, undulating desert, with now and again a few thorny trees to break the skyline.

It was becoming hotter, and during the short stop the compartment had become like an oven. On the horizon the fat, cumulus clouds built up into mountains of gleaming white, but overhead the sky was clear and of a rich blue.

The swaying of the train lulled us into a dreamy void, and we sat looking dreamily through the window. The scene was unchanging. Alan woke suddenly, looked around him, and said "Where are we?" Tim grunted. "In the middle of the Bundu." "First time I've been so far north," said Alan. "We shan't be far from the Limpopo." He yawned, and stretched.

"What the hell's the Limpopo?" asked Tim. "River, man." Alan went on, "Never heard of the Limpopo? It's full of crocodiles. Dead dangerous. Some pupes force landed near there, once. They didn't know about the crocs, and went in for a swim. Those crocs have a grip of iron once they get hold of you. You've had it if they do. And their tails. They can break every bone in your body with a single lash."

"Nice country you've got here," commented Barker, "What happened to the pupils?" "They both got too close to the crocs. One was killed immediately, the other got his leg almost bitten off, but managed to crawl back to the kite. He lay there bleeding and suffering for six hours, and went off his nut. They saved his leg, and about a year later he got his wings." "Yeah?" said Tim cryptically. "Yep."

At that moment the compartment door flew open again, and someone shouted, "Pontoon school starting up – anyone coming?" I looked across at Tim, and asked him if he would like a game. He shook his head. "Come on," I said, "you've just been paid. Now's your chance to make a bit. Let's go and have a couple of hands." He agreed reluctantly, and we left the compartment. The game was already in progress a few compartments down, and soon we were struggling over a heap of legs and arms to an upturned suitcase which was being used as the card table.

An hour later we struggled out of the smoky atmosphere, and gasped for breath at an open window. "I think we're just pulling in," said Tim, "there's a water drop coming up. How much have you got?" I counted the loose change in my pocket. "One and four-pence," I admitted. "Two bob, me" said Tim, "and an English six-pence. And only a fortnight to go to payday. You're a bright boy. You and your Pontoon." I laughed. "Well, there is always the old moneylender Barker, you know." Tim sniffed. "I'm going back. I think I'll have a hunk of that chocolate to take my mind of it."

We went back to the compartment. Barker looked at us in disgust, and Alan grinned.
"Well, that passed the journey for you gentlemen," said Alan. "I think we're coming in." Tim took down his sun helmet and fished round for the chocolate. With a grasp of dismay he pulled out his hand. It was covered in chocolate. So was the inside of the helmet, which Tim flung on the floor in annoyance.

"Look at that," he said, "Bloody choc and my topee ruined. You and your damned Pontoon." I smiled at him with glee. "Barker?" I said. "Huh?"
I leaned over, offering a packet. "Have a cigarette, old chap," I said, and felt relieved when he took one. He had accepted the time honoured system of the opening of negotiations.

Chapter 9

My new instructor shook my hand. He was a Pilot Officer, having gone through the ranks right up to Warrant Officer, before being commissioned. He was about twenty-three, had flown in the Battle of Britain, had flown over Germany and Libya and was now having a rest from operations.

"I hope you like it here," he said. "Have you been inside an oxford?" I told him that I had not, and he showed me over the aircraft. It is a twin-engine trainer, with two seats at the front side-by-side, and each fitted with controls. The pupil sits on the left, and there is also a bomb bay for photography, and practise bombing. The controls and knobs and levers, instruments, and gadgets all looked complicated, and I doubted if I ever should master them.

He told me to sit in the seat and try the controls. They felt heavy after the delicate controls of the Tiger Moth, but the basic elements were the same, and he assured me that I should have little trouble with the aircraft. "You'll enjoy flying these," he said. "And make the most of it. This is the last time you'll be able to enjoy your flying. The next time you are on conversion you'll have other things to think about besides flying, and you won't notice it as much."

The instructor was evidently very keen at his job, and loved the Oxford, for he showed me every detail of the aircraft, explained how it behaved in the air, and on the ground when taxiing, and its idiosyncrasies, which aeroplanes, like people, have. He explained about the twin throttles, flaps, the retractable undercarriage, the warning lights for the wheels and so much more. I assimilated some of it, and hoped to pick up the rest in due course.

He told me to go and draw a parachute. A South African WAAF signed it out to me, and I clumped out to the aircraft with it swinging like an enormous tail. The cabin of this Oxford, which had been standing on the tarmac like a greenhouse, was hot. Whilst my instructor explained just what he was going to do, the perspiration streamed down both of us in rivers.

I was glad when the engines were started, and he motioned me to open the side window. A glorious stream of cooler air bathed my face, and when the chocks were waved away the instructor taxied out from the tarmac. I watched his every movement. He opened one throttle for a turn, pressed a small switch attached to the control column, and I heard a whoosh. This was the brakes helping to effect the turn. He opened the throttles wider; the aeroplane sprinted along, the instructor keeping it straight by judicious use of throttle, aileron, rudder and brake. He looked as though he was playing a Wurlitzer at the Odeon.

"You must not taxi like this," he was saying, "no more than five miles an hour. I'm just doing it to save time." He bought the aircraft to a stop cross wind, and turned to me. "Now we shall do the vital actions. TMPFF –

Throttle, Mixture, Pitch, Fuel, Flaps."

As he reeled them off one by one, he checked each control, then turned into the wind, opened the throttles, and we skimmed along the ground. The noise was deafening, as the needle showed full boost of the engine, but the take-off was soon affected, and we were at three hundred feet, when I saw him touch the lever to retract the undercarriage. He did a circuit, and I watched him as he pointed the revs out to me, the speeds, the heights, the oil pressure, and the trimming procedure.

Now the throttles had been pushed back it was much quieter, and there was no more noise than that of a high powered car. This sensation of flying in an enclosed cockpit suited me. It was comfortable. One had room to move, and a far better view from the cockpit than the Tiger Moth had.

"I am going to do a wheels landing," the instructor said. "I should stick to that until you get the feel of her. Don't try a three pointer for a while." He took the aircraft in, held it off a few from the ground, and gradually lowered in onto the wheels. It was perfect, and there was no sensation of landing, as the tail sank gradually, and we rolled to a stop at the end of the field. While taxiing back he explained to me the Vital actions for landing which were remembered by the mnemonics BUMPFF – Brakes Undercart, Mixture, Pitch, Fuel and Flaps.

"Never land with your brakes on, "he said, "And for heaven's sake, remember to lower you undercart. If you don't, and you throttle back, the warning lights show, coupled with a hooting from the klaxon horn. But even so we still get bods coming in without lowering the undercart."

I refrained from saying that it would be a stupid thing to do, for it sounded as though it was the very thing that I would do before long. We took off again, and climbed to about five thousand feet. The instructor handed over to me to get the feel of the aircraft in straight and level flight. Once trimmed the Oxford flew herself, and I had a good look at the surrounding countryside. There was a small range of mountains in the distant haze, and one or two dusty looking roads which appeared to lead to nowhere.

Now and again I could make out a small village – a few pointed huts with small figures moving around them. No roads led to or from them, and they looked primitive, and were probably as backward as any jungle village. To the north I saw a white ribbon winding through a maze of dense green. I pointed out to the instructor.

"The Limpopo river," he said. "Later on you will be flying over it on a navigation exercise." He took over control of the aeroplane, turned her south, and began losing height rapidly doing stall turns on the way. "Not part of the course, but fun, and it does show you what an Oxford can do. Watch this Immelman turn."

I watched, but had no idea what he was doing. The aircraft reared gently, seemed to hover for a moment in mid-air, and then suddenly the nose dropped sharply, and I thought we would go into a spin. But it was a perfectly executed manoeuvre, and there was no discomfort as we swept almost vertically downward and gradually pulled out.

The instructor took out a map from his pocket. A portion was encircled in violet. "This is the low flying area. I'm going to show you the boundaries now, so try to follow on the map," he said, "This is the only area in which we are allowed to do low flying. Don't on any account fly low over any other part of the country. If you do, you're for the high jump, make no mistake."

I looked at the map, and the instructor pointed to a road ahead. I found it easily on the map, and orientated it in the direction in which we were headed. He came down to twenty feet, and gradually the heat drifted into the cockpit. He went lower, fixed the airspeed at two hundred knots, and concentrated on the rough terrain which came at us in waves. He was constantly moving the stick, and had his hand on the throttle. "It's very easy to misjudge height so near the deck" he shouted, still looking straight ahead. "Never take your eyes off the ground for a moment. If you have to, pull back slightly on the stick."

The ground whooshed by in a continuous blur – rough dry desert, broken now and again by the flash of white from a dried up river bed or a crusted road, or broken perhaps by a sudden black patch of a native compound. Now and again I could see an animal running as though for its life in a zig zag pattern. I could not make out what the animals were.

The low flying was exhilarating, and I could see that the instructor enjoyed it. It was probably the only bit of excitement in an otherwise monotonous existence, for I believed that all instructors got bored.

When he suddenly pulled back on the stick and gave the aircraft more throttle I looked for a pinpoint on the map again. I found it. A railway line. I looked down. There was no mistaking the glint of the sun on the rails.

We flew back to the airfield, joined the circuit and landed. "How do you like the Oxford?" my instructor asked as we unloosened our parachute harnesses. "Very nice," I replied. "I enjoyed the flight, sir." "Good, we'll get down to work tomorrow then. Circuits and bumps. I want you off solo quickly."

I walked from the airfield feeling that I was going to enjoy my stay here. I liked my instructor, and I liked the Oxford. I felt confident, much more confident than I had felt when flying Tiger Moths, and I put it down to the treatment I had received from the instructor. He had spoken more as man-to-man, which was music to me after the rather patronising air of my other instructor. That was the flying buttoned up, I thought. I was going to enjoy this. But what of the ground subjects? What of the Wings Exam?

I met Tim in the YMCA canteen. He was drinking a Coca Cola and eating an extremely sticky cake. "You look full of beans," he whipped. I told him of my trip, and the instructor. "One of the best is P.O. Thwaites," I said. "Good," Tim replied, "He's my instructor too, I hear. My turn tomorrow." "You'll like him, Tim. Your type, and seeing that we've got him for some twenty weeks, it's a good thing."

Alan Afton joined us. He had just come down, and was brimming with the same enthusiasm. We talked shop as though we were old hands, comparing noted and experiences.

"Christ," said Tim, "anyone would think you two had just been through the Wings Exam…" "Funny you should say that, man," Alan broke in, "I've just been talking to a friend of mine from Kimberley. He's just finished taking his Wings Exam, says it's a piece of cake. There he is, over there." Alan shouted, and a very smart South African came over. "I've just been telling these Rafs that you've taken your Wings Exam today, Bill."

The South African grinned. "Finished today, you mean." "Lucky bounder," said Tim.

"Soon be up north, now," said Bill, "Another few weeks, a spot of leave, and then – whoosh – the desert."

"Fancy anyone wanting to go up to the desert," I exclaimed.

"I'd go to the North pole to see a bit of action," said Bill, and I think he meant it.

We piled the questions on to him. We wanted to know every detail of the Wings Exam, for this was the first time that we had been able to tackle anyone for first class information, and coming so fresh from the ordeal he was bound to remember everything.

"Sorry chaps," Bill said suddenly, "I've got to go now. I'm going to the bio. Tell you what, though, come round to my billet tomorrow night, and I'll give you all the gen. In fact," he laughed, "I'll share out my cribs with you."

"Well, Tim," I said when Bill had gone, "it seems that are some decent SAAF's." "The best, man, is bill," said Alan, "and for that crack you can buy me a coke."

Chapter 10

The next day I was not flying, and spent a full day in lectures. In the morning we had a navigation lecture, in a hot class room, where it was difficult not to drop asleep. The lecturer was Flight Lieutenant Moss DFC, who thankfully seasoned his lecture with anecdotes of his operational experiences, though not in a boastful fashion.

This first lecture was mostly concerned with revision of work we had previously done, and we scribbled furiously in our notebooks. I was thankful when it was over, and we move into an armament lecture room to learn about guns, and the trajectory of bombs. After this lecture there was a tea break, followed by a meteorology lecture and a film on the weather, and to round off the morning the most interesting lecture of them all so far – signals – where, with something to do in the nature of sending and receiving Morse code the eyelids did not droop so readily. During the afternoon we had only two classes, more navigation, and a talk on pyrotechnics.

This was to be the pattern for our long stay here, varied sometimes by half a day flying, and the other on lectures, and sometimes one or even two days flying unbroken by lectures. We all naturally preferred the flying, but were terribly keen to learn all the ground stuff thoroughly, which may have been dry and boring on the ground, but was so closely allied to flying, and would one day be so much a part of our everyday duties that the two were really inseparable. Besides there was a Wings Exam to think of.

We finished the last lecture at about four, and went to the YCMA for the usual Cokes and buns. Glen Phillips, the little sergeant, who had been made our flight leader, sat in front of me.

"I've found out something very interesting today," he said. "Oh?" "Yes, I saw it yesterday when I was up, and decided to explore it." "What is it?" I asked.

Glen wrinkled his face, in a frown of concentration and explained, "A river. There is a river near here – a dried up one. It looked interesting from the air, and I made a few discreet enquiries about it today." "What did you find out?" "Well," he went on, "I'm told that its banks are full of lush tropical fruits, and I thought, well – I though I might get up an expedition, and wander out to sample them." "You mean walk?" He nodded. "There's no other way. But I reckon it would be well worth it. It's just full of fruit – stuff you can't buy here." "Can't you get enough fruit in the Padre's Pub?" I asked, meaning a small store that the Padre ran on a non profit basis, and which he himself called his pub.

"He can't get the kind of stuff that is there," went on Glen, "This is tropical – the real fruit, lovely fruit you've never even heard of, never mind tasted." "Some of it might be poison, you know." I added. "I thought of that. There is a sure way of finding out, though. It never fails." "Oh, what's that then?"

Phillips blandly replied, "Eat it – we'll soon know. Anyway, are you with me?" "Sorry," I replied, "I've some swotting to do. Besides, I've arranged to go round to see a bloke who has just taken his Wings Exam to get the gen." "We've only just arrived. You don't want to start swotting yet." "It's never too early for me to start, Glen," I replied. "Tell you what we'll do," he said, sucking the bottom of his Coca Cola bottle through his straw, "We'll go exploring and swot on the way. You ask me questions, and I'll ask you. And we'll be back for dinner, easy."

I agreed, and Glen rubbed his hands. "Number one on the expedition," he said, and went off to look for more members. I went to my billet to change, and Glen called for me a quarter of an hour later. He was scowling, and I laughed when he said nobody was interested. "They're all a lot of stick in the muds," he said, "bashing their beds, that's all they think of. No spirit of adventure."

"An old man like you shouldn't be thinking of adventure, anyway," I ventured, "you ought to be on your bed nursing your varicose veins." I looked down at his legs covered in the longs shorts he always wore. They were truly the most gnarled, knobbly and ugliest legs I had ever seen. "The finest limbs in this hemisphere," Glen said seriously, lifting his shorts a trifle. "Mind you don't burn them," I said, and he grinned, for there was exactly one inch between his shorts and khaki stockings.

We moved out of the billet, Glen still grumbling because he had found no more recruits. As we walked through the billet lines I heard someone singing in an awful monotone;
Where be that blackbird to
I know where he be
He be up the apple tree
And I be arter he.

I went inside the billet of George Marsden. He was standing in his vest stroking his thin moustache. "Come on," I said, "we're going hunting."

Solemnly George put on a shirt, shorts, and shoes and followed me outside. "See how easy it is?" I said to Glen. "I've brought a minstrel with us. He's going to serenade us."
George immediately began his song about the blackbird, and we walked out of the camp into the bush.

We walked quite a distance before we eventually came to the river bank. At this point it was wide, and the banks were devoid of anything living. The earth was crumbled, and yellow, and powdered under our feet as we slipped down its banks. "An interesting case of soil erosion," said Phillips. "Where be that blackbird to…." sang Marsden.

The river bottom had once been clay, but was now a hard reddish mass of stone. It looked as though water had never flowed through, but Phillips assured me that last year it was in flood, hence a good crop of tropical vegetation this year.

"Where?" I asked, for there was not one single green blade of grass even, anywhere in sight. "Probably round the next corner," he said doggedly. "Rivers have bends, not corners," remarked Marsden.

We reached the next bend, and still there was nothing. When we had rounded it we seemed to be miles from anywhere, and it was extremely quiet. Now and again a brightly plumed bird would fly startled from the banks, and once we heard the chatter of a large bird which looked like an eagle, but Phillips explained it was a vulture.

"Where be that vulture to…" sang Marsden. "If I come across a snake, Marsden, I'll curl the damned thing round your neck," said Phillips ominously. "Did you have to bring this poor man's Bing Crosby?"

We marched on, and the going became harder. The river bed was covered in small boulders now, and Phillips suggested that we look out for scorpions and snakes.

We searched the banks for signs of the lush tropical fruit that we had been promised, but Phillips seemed quite happy as he turned over stones looking for livestock. The banks were still deserted, the yellow dust everywhere, and they were so high now that it was impossible to see over the tops of them, and when we tried to climb the banks all we got was a shoe full of this soft powder.

Phillips did find a scorpion, but it bolted from him, and hid under an unmoveable rock.

"He's gone to fetch his family," said Marsden, "Come on, let's get going." We left Phillips prodding the rock, and walked on ahead. "He's bloody mad," said Marsden, "there's no fruit here. Somebody's been pulling his…"

"Look!" I shouted.

We had rounded another bend, and in front of us stretched a long line of brown bushes on each side of the bank, growing grotesquely from the dust. We could make out whether they were fruit bushes, it seemed very unlikely, but we shouted to Phillips, and he came crashing up the river bed. As soon as he saw the bushes he smirked, "what did I tell you? Exotic blooms of the tropics." "Bull," said George, "They're weeds in the Bundu" and he seemed right, as when we examined them closer we found hard spiky thorns and nothing else. Even these thorns broke off as we handled them, and the bushes seemed dead.

But Phillips was not dismayed. "This is just the start of it," he explained. He pointed to a tree in the distance. "Look, there's a tree, and it's got some fruit on." Sure enough, a little further along, rising from the prickly bushes stood a thin tree, and little globes of some kind of fruit or vegetable hung from its branches.

We examined it closely, and Phillips reached down some of the fruit. "Prickly pears," he said, "I've heard about them." He handed the fruit round. They looked like figs, and had a skin which we were told to peel off. I watched Phillips peeling his pear, and then he began to eat. I peeled one and bit into it. Immediately my tongue felt like it had been jabbed by a thousand needles.

"You didn't peel enough off," said Phillips, "try this."

I tried his pear, but again got the prickly sensation. I flung it away. "Don't you like this tropical fruit?" "If that's all you can offer, no." I said. "There'll be some more further on." "Keep it," I replied. Phillips looked a little disgruntled. "Who told you about this tropical fruit?" I asked him. "Alan Afton."

George broke out in a fit of laughter. "That duff gen merchant! Didn't he tell you that you could get a boat down here as well?" "Well if Alan told you, its no good going any further," I suggested, "there won't be anything else." "Better than sitting swotting," grumbled Phillips. "Hey, I almost forgot about that," I said, "let's start. And let's get weaving. I'm going to get all the gen on the Wings Exam tonight."

We asked and answered questions in the form of a quiz all the way back to camp. I think I learned more from Glen about airframes and engines than from all the instructors I had had so far. He had that uncanny knack of explaining something highly technical in the simplest language, and of knowing whether a point was grasped. And undoubtedly he knew his stuff. He had been directly concerned with airframes and engines for ten years.

We walked towards our billet, and saw a group standing outside the wash-house. I recognised Tim and Alan. "There's your man, Phillips," I said to Glen, but he was already on his way over to Alan.

But Alan spoke first "Bill's bought it," he said. "How do you mean, Bill's bought it?" I asked. Alan slapped his pockets, as though searching for a cigarette. "He piled in this afternoon. Low flying, along with his instructor, and another pupil." "Bull," I said. "No, it's true." Tim put in. "All three were killed."

I felt as shaken as they looked. This was our first serious accident, and it seemed unbelievable. Tim nodded at me, "You and Alan are two of the pall bearers," he said.

That was the first time, and the only time, that I wished sincerely to never fly again.

Chapter 11

Opposite my name in the Authorisation book I saw I was scheduled for an hour's solo practising precautionary landings. I decided to practise these at the civil aerodrome, which was little used, and would be quieter than the main one. It was a beautifully clear and calm day, and I swung myself into the seat with a song in my heart. I took off, and headed towards the town, and flew over it looking down and picking out the Jacaranda lined street. It was a blaze of purple interspersed with a flash of white from the houses, all clean and very beautiful.

But I had to keep my mind on the business at hand. Precautionary landings. These were landings where had the minimum of power allowed, and consisted of an extremely flat approach, simulating a landing with engine trouble, when one was 'nursing' the engine, and with only a small landing area. The idea was to put the aircraft down on the nearest possible position to the edge of the field, and come to a stop in an extremely short run.

I approached the airfield, came down to a couple of hundred feet, gave some flap and power and held her at a speed just about stalling. I lost height very slowly, popped over the fence, cut the engine, and landed neatly in the three point position. Almost immediately I applied brake, and the aircraft trundled to a stop. Very nice; about the best I had ever done. I wished that my instructor had been with me. I made a mental note of the position at which I had actually stopped, decided to try and better it, and took off again.

This time I made my approach even shallower, and sank the aircraft slower so that I was almost flying into the field. Just on the fence I saw a sudden flash of yellow underneath me. Involuntarily I slammed on full throttle, kicked the rudder, and slewed over. The flash of yellow loomed near, and I closed my eyes waiting for the impact.

I felt the aircraft slipping, kicked on correcting rudder, and she heeled over. For a split second there was no sign of the other aircraft, and then the ground came up. I cut the throttle, heaved back on the stick, and the aircraft sank to a perfect landing.

And then, only a few yards away, cutting right across my landing run I saw the other aircraft. I pressed the brakes hard, and pulled on the stick to keep the nose from going over. The aircraft bucked up, I let off the brake, and the tail went down again. I was nearer the other aircraft, and saw the quick scared look the pilot gave me. I pressed the brake again, felt the nose go up, but held the brake, until she almost keeled over. Mercifully, the other pilot had given his kite a quick burst of throttle, and we missed colliding by a hairsbreadth.

I trundled to a stop, and the perspiration started pouring from me. I turned quickly across wing, and then slumped over the stick. My head was reeling. That I had not seen the other plane was astounding. That I had got away with it when so near to him was nothing short of a miracle. I wiped the sweat from my face, as the other aircraft drew alongside me. I recognised the pilot. It was a SAAF pupil, and he looked as shaken as I felt.

He looked across at me, his face pale and strained, and smiled sympathetically. I gave him the thumbs up again, thankful that he had not an instructor with him. He motioned with his hand and I saw another aircraft landing; I prayed that it had no instructor.

I stood until he landed meaning to take off again as quickly as I could, and keeping a wary eye on the plane that had just landed. Everything seemed quite normal, and I congratulated myself that the pilot had not seen the occurrence.

But as soon as the plane had stopped, and turned crosswind, an arm encased in white coveralls snaked out of the instructor's window, and a long finger beckoned me. He taxied quickly to the boundary, and I followed like a delinquent following a policeman. I still could not see who the instructor was, but hoped that it was one that I knew, and one who would give me a good talking to, but not report me. A report at this stage might mean goodbye to my wings forever.

I left the aircraft ticking over, undid my 'chute harness, and went over to the plane. A pupil sat demurely by the side of the instructor, who turned as I climbed in. Me heart missed a beat, when I saw who it was. The Wing Commander. The Flying Pencil, a stickler for discipline, and a noted washer out of pupils. "This is it," I thought.

He asked me my name. "Right," he said, "Go back to the airfield, and report to your flight. You are grounded on my orders." His words lashed me as though they were delivered with a whip. The quiet 'you are grounded' was like a death knell.

I could have cried as I took the aircraft back to the main field, and sought out my instructor. After the initial he talked it over with me, and promised to see what he could do, but added that he was only a P.O. "Couldn't you have chosen anybody else?" he asked, "the only important person on the station, and you have to almost write yourself and another person off in front of him?"

I was very popular in the mess in an infamous way. A group soon gathered round me at lunch time, having heard the other pupil's version.

The SAAF pupil came across to me. He shook his head, "Golly, it was close," he said. "I felt almost as much to blame as you are – so if there's anything I can do by way of explanation, let me know." "I still can't understand how it happened," I replied, "I must have been in a dream." "These things do happen, don't they? I suppose you'll get a ticking off from the Wingco, and that'll be that. It could have been worse, and if you hadn't taken that violent evasive action we'd both have had it. I didn't know you were there, until I look round after landing."

He was decent about it, but of course, he was in no way to blame, one cannot see upwards and backwards in an Oxford.

The SAAF pupil was about the only sympathetic person there. The rest had me clapped in irons, court martialled, dismissed the service, and selling matches in the street for the rest of the duration. Even Tim made tentative enquires about the next person to move into the billet when I had gone.

I felt a bit better after all the chaffing, if they had all behaved in the way the SAAF pupil had done I should have felt very depressed. However I felt miserable enough when the whole course was flying in the afternoon, and I stretched myself out in the quiet billet, listening to the maddening drone of the aircraft as they took off and landed.

When Tim came in after the day's flying he asked, "Well, packed up yet?" He had news for me. I was to appear on a charge the following morning for contravening SAAF standing orders. I would go before the C.O – a Colonel.

This was confirmed by my instructor a little later who came as though to serve an official summons. "Put your best blue on," he said, "and polish your buttons, and your shoes. And good luck, there's nothing I can do."

I spent an extremely unhappy evening with the charge hanging over my head, and I kept thinking, 'oh well, it will all be over by tomorrow.' But this didn't comfort me at all, and I spend a very sleepless night worrying.

In the morning I woke very early, and did my last bit of spit and polish, and went up to the C.O's block, where I was to await my escort. A Corporal who I knew fairly well came up to me and explained the procedure. I must stand to attention the whole time, not speak until spoken to, and then only answer yes or no. "And whatever you do, Noble," he said, "accept the C.O's punishment, whatever it is. Now, give me your cap."

I had heard about this giving up one's cap, and confirmed with him that it was only traditional. It was taken away during the old days so that the prisoner would not fling it at the C.O. He would have done so when caps were made of metal, and spiky, and not soft forage caps, much damage would have been done.

And then I heard the words, "Prisoner, attention!" I was the only prisoner there that morning, and stood to attention in my very best manner, which was passable, even to the Corporal, but only just. "When you get inside, smarten up." He whispered.

When I faced the Colonel I found it hard to look directly at him. His eyes seemed to be piercing me. However, I held my head high, and felt a bit of a martyr, for I was pleading guilty.

The charge was read out, comments made by the Wing Commander, and then I was asked if I had anything to add. I replied that I had not. I wished that they would get to the end of it, and tell me what my sentence was. After a long half hour, at which everyone seemed to be speaking but me I heard the CO address me. I had a most beautiful strip torn off, and when he had finished I felt as though I was the lowest thing that had crept from a hole.

The awful part about it was that everything he said was perfectly true, but it sounded much worse coming from him, and in language couched in legal terms. I still held my head high, however, and waited for his last words. They came, and I learned that for my offence I would be confined to camp for 14 days and would have my flying log book endorsed. I also learned that I was very lucky to get away with such a light sentence and that in future I must be careful, and that any other flying offence would not be dealt with so leniently.

I was marched out, and given my cap back. The Corporal told me to report to the guardroom immediately. I was much relieved, but worried a little about the endorsement of my log book. However, I decided that it might be forgotten about, as no one had mentioned it, and I was sure that it was not the concern of the Corporal.

I went to the guard room at the Main gate, and reported to the Sergeant. I told him the story, and he made me welcome. "You'll have to do fatigues," he said, "it's usually cookhouse, but we might find you something cushy. I don't like putting pupils in the cookhouse."

I thanked him and told him that I didn't mind, but he said he did and would arrange something decent. "Report tonight after lectures or flying or whatever you're doing."

The attitude of most of my friends was one of disappointment. They would have enjoyed something more drastic and sensational, and it seemed that I had let them all down with this anti-climax. However they hoped that I would enjoy the fatigues.

My cushy job turned out to be waste paper collector. I was to go over the whole camp picking up litter, and was provided with a stick with a spike on the end. It was good healthy open air work, and I gave up when my stick became full, partly because I made it spin out so long that it was always dark by the time it was full.

My appearance round the pupil's billets was always greeted with hoots of derision, and I often had a crowd following me offering advice, or scattering more litter in my wake. Undeterred, I carried on, wondering whether I wouldn't have done better in the cookhouse after all.

One evening I was at the usual job near the Main gate when I saw my instructor coming. I bent low over my stick and turned my back to him. But he recognised me, and called me to him.

"What on god's earth are you doing?" he asked. "I'm the champion paper picker upper," I replied flippantly. "Good lord, you shouldn't be doing that!" "Oh, I don't mind. Its fatigues and a darn sight easier than peeling potatoes," I told him. "You're on a technical offence. You can't do fatigues when you're on a technical offence. Come on, we'll go and see the Sergeant." We marched in to the Sergeant, and the instructor explained to him.

The Sergeant scratched his head. "You're quite right, sir" he said, "But I had no idea he was on a technical offence. Of course he mustn't do that sort of thing," he apologised to me and asked for my stick. "Just report once at night, that's all you have to do if you're on a technical offence." I thanked my instructor for intervening, and thanked the Sergeant for the cushy job, and for now finishing my punishment. I was pleased that I only had to report at the Guard Room in future.

I went back to the billet to tell my friends the good news. It was the thirteenth night of my fourteen confined to camp, and that same day my log book had been endorsed in large red words as though written in blood...

Chapter 12

Two days before the Wings Parade I still had six hours flying to do. "Don't panic," said Tim smugly. "I'm not panicking," I replied "but six hours is a long time. What if the weather clamps in and there's no flying?" "Christ, John, we've been here for twenty weeks and the weather hasn't clamped in once! Why should it now? Go to it, boy, go to it." "Are you coming down to the flight?" I asked. "Not on your life," he grinned. "The next thing I do officially is to sling one up when the old man give me my Wings."

I walked down to the Flight hut alone. One or two aircraft were being revved up, but all was quiet in 'A' Flight. "Here he comes, my only customer," said the solitary WAAF timekeeper as I went into the office.

I was detailed for a cross-country trip, solo, landing at an Air School some three hours flying away. I had already done this trip once, so I was happy about it – it was better than six hours circuits and bumps, and it was up to me to see that all the six hours were wiped off at one go ."Where are all the instructors?" I asked. "In bed, probably" she replied. "One or two of them came down to see if anything was cooking, and P.O. Thwaites came down to fill in the book for your detail, and that's about all I've seen."

I calculated that I should be back in time for a last night out in town, for tomorrow night would see us all busy packing. "Better nip up and see the Duty pilot," I heard the WAAF say.

Lieutenant Parrish, the Duty Pilot, was sitting in his little box on stilts sucking an orange. "Delighted to see you," he said, "You're the pupil for the cross country?"

He pushed a notice into my hands. It listed restricted areas, low flying areas and places of high ground. I signed a book to show anyone interested that I had read the notice. A weather report slid along the table. "There'll be high cu. this afternoon, possibly cu.nim. and thunderstorms. Watch out." I signed for the report and forecast, and was given a list of emergency landing grounds. They were all north of the Limpopo, so I didn't see the point, but I signed for them all the same. The Duty Pilot gave me a sheaf of papers. "That's all the bumpf you'll need, I'll signal your destination, and they'll keep you a lunch ready."

The aircraft swung easily off the runway. I climbed to 6,000 feet and set the course on the compass and direction Indicator. It was cooler at that height, and the steady throb of the engines lulled me into a watchful daydream. There was nothing to do, but keep an eye on the speed, height, oil pressure, revs and petrol, with an occasional glance at the compass to confirm that 'red was still on red' every twenty minutes or so; I also re-set the direction indicator, and checked it.

The ground below presented a vast sameness, and the only unbroken thing was the orange grove which skipped beneath the aircraft at almost the same time that I had pinpointed it on the map.

I saw the airfield ten minutes before landing, and now I looked out for the boys in the single-seater aircraft, who, I was told, were 'high spirited' and not above 'buzzing' a visiting aircraft

However I saw none until I joined the circuit for landing, and then they seemed to be humming around like flies. Their circuit seemed to be as busy as ours was at lunch time. As a visiting pupil I was an object of interest in the mess, which I noticed was much noisier than our own mess. A buck-toothed pupil led me to one side and shook me by asking for details of crashes at my school. "We hold the record, you know," he said proudly. I congratulated him, and assured him that it was an unenviable one.

I was glad when it was time to go, for I felt strangely out of place, and I took off again at two o'clock.

There was a head wind and I concluded that I would be home a little after 5, for I had been briefed to fly the return journey at the same airspeed.

The orange groves came up on my port side instead of directly underneath, and I altered my course a few degree to compensate, assuming that the wind direction had changed slightly and that I was drifting to starboard a little more than I expected. I crossed a road shortly after leaving the orange groves and pinpointed it on the map. In front I watched the cumulus cloud building up into magnificent towers of shimmering white.

After half an hour's flying the bumps started. I strapped myself in and trimmed the aircraft nose heavy to ease the fatigue on my arms, the bumps became worse, and in some of them I lost or gained five hundred feet in a few seconds. The cloud in front became nearer and darker in colour and I saw that I would have to reduce height. When I could see the swirl of the cloud I eased back on the throttle, and kept the same airspeed and course, gradually losing height without altering my flight plan.

The huge, billowing clouds seemed in turmoil as I came nearer to them – they swirled and heaved, sometimes enveloping the aircraft completely, but it seemed that I was going to get beneath the base before I few into the middle of them.

I saw another road below, and searched vainly for it on the map, but it was not marked. The map was dancing about now as the aircraft bucked, and I wished I had bought a knee clip.

Large spots of rain hit the front windscreen. And immediately I was in cloud. The bumps got worse, and I transferred all my attention to the blind flying panel. I kept the aircraft level, although I had the feeling as I always did when blind flying that the aircraft was heeling over to port.

I saw the direction indicator whirling round madly. I had forgotten to re-set it, and the gyro would not now work for some minutes. I re-set it, and watched the compass needle; it was quivering like a mad thing, and it was impossible to steer a straight course by it. Better to rely on the turn and back indicator and try not to skid. I throttled back and thrust down the nose, maintaining the same airspeed. This would reduce height more quickly. There was no sensation of movement whatsoever, apart from the bumps. The aircraft seemed to be buffeting crazily in a thousand tons of tightly pack cotton wool as the cloud got thicker.

The altimeter needle went round unceasingly. I was down to four thousand feet now, and still in cloud. Three thousand, five hundred and it was as dense as ever. I dared not go very much lower as four thousand was the minimum height I was scheduled to fly at because of high ground. The bumps became fiercer, and it was impossible to hold that height. The wings were flapping like a screaming bird. My hands were sweating on the control column. I feared that very soon something would break, as the column was snatched out of my hands time and time again.

I put on full throttle and climbed. Nothing happened – no height was gained at all. In fact the aircraft appeared to be sinking. I lowered the airspeed to almost stalling point and put on full boost. Still nothing happened. And the altimeter needle flickered gently – downwards – and it crept dangerously towards three thousand feet. At any minute I expected the sound of ripping metal and fought like a madman to keep the nose up and the speed above stalling point.

And then suddenly I started going up – very rapidly, as though in a lift. The altimeter needle shivered, and then reversed its previous journey. Height was put on with a speed that made my ears sing and in no time was registering 6,000 feet again. I throttled back and heaved a large sigh of relief. This was short lived when I noticed light patches on the windscreen which flaked off, only to be replaced by more. Ice. I looked at the wings. All along the leading edges was thick white ice, which broke off in huge chunks. This really was something to worry about. I climbed, hoping tat I would reach a warmer layer of air, but the ice had built up, until the aircraft became heavy and even more difficult to control.   I was faced with the problem of sticking there until the weight became so heavy that the aircraft would not fly any more and would drop like a stone, or whether to risk going down to warmer air where there was the ground – somewhere – in the nature of small mountain peaks.

I had no choice; the aircraft was losing height again, despite the full throttle that I made. As I descended the ice broke away, and as it broke off and became lighter I was caught in an upward current again. I throttled back completely, and put the nose down, and managed, by riding the bumps and the upward currents, to lose some height. It was a slow business, and at 3,500 feet my arms arched. Still it sank, and again wrenched and buffeted endlessly.

Suddenly it became lighter, and I was out of the cloud. Below me I could make out no peaks but only the outlines of a town. I lost height and encircled the town, looking for a landmark. I could not find anything at all, and I had no idea where I was. I descended to a thousand feet, but still couldn't recognise anything. I put my flaps down and circled slowly. A few people came out of their houses and waved, doubtless collecting my number.

It was hopeless. I was completely lost. There was nothing I could pinpoint; I could not even find the station. I had no idea in which direction he camp lay. I decided to land. I found a field fairly near to the town, and looked it over from a low height, before making a circuit over it. I put down my wheels, and throttled back.

And then I remembered. In two days time I was to receive my Wings. But not if I landed here, that would be certain. There would perhaps be a court of inquiry; there would certainly be a long delay in my getting away from a place like this town. "No" I shouted, "You've had me." I put on full throttle, pulled up the nose, and retracted the undercarriage.

I looked for a road leading out of the town, and decided to follow it. It wound and turned, but I stuck to it, now and again losing it as the low cloud enveloped me occasionally.

I followed this road for about half an hour. Visibility ahead and to the sides of me was very poor, but I soon noticed that the sky above me was much lighter, and with a sigh of relief I glimpsed blue. I immediately began climbing, keeping an eye on the road below. At 6,000 feet everything was calm again, and the holocaust I had just flown through appeared only as white and shining clouds. I climbed to 10,000 feet, and then, well to my starboard, I pinpointed a familiar landmark. I still could not make out the road I had followed on the map, or the town I had flown over.

I raced towards the landmark, and set my course from there, puzzling all the back just where I had been. I found it very difficult to work out, though, and decided to forget about it, and have a go at getting sorted for landing.

I landed with about ten minutes to spare, my tanks registering empty. The low flying that I had down now worried me. I decided to report it to the Duty Pilot, and sign the low flying book, which I hoped would put me in the clear.

"Glad you came," he said," If you hadn't I should have had to send for you." "I've come to report unauthorised low flying, sir," I said. "I know about it. No fewer than ten people have reported you by phone." "Where was I, sir?" I asked. He looked at me blankly, "Where were you? Didn't you know?" I explained to him what happened. "Good Lord," he went on, "You mean you were stooging round the in cloud at that height!" He mentioned the name of a town, and I felt my legs go weak. "That town," he said, "is surrounded by mountains 7,000 feet high, with only one narrow pass in and out. How did you get away with it?" shakily I told him I didn't know.

Chapter 13

The day of the Wings Parade I awoke with an aching head and a sniffling cold. But there was no time to enjoy my suffering, for we were on parade early. Tim was still sprawled under his mosquito net without a stitch on him when I awoke, and as he stretched himself out he looked much worse than I felt, for the previous night he had been on a bender. He recovered when I told him what day it was.

There was complete silence in our billet as we prepared ourselves for the parade. Tim couldn't find his best blue, and then remembered with horror that he had left it in somebody else's billet last night. Somebody had promised to clean it for him, but he couldn't remember who it was. He flew out of the hut, and I heard him banging on every billet door in the line.

Meanwhile, I polished my own buttons until they shone, took out some heavy books from on top of my collar, and a clean flash which had been pressing there for a week, and took my trousers from underneath the mattress which had been pressing there for twenty weeks. I disregarded the fine mesh on the cloth which had pressed into them, and hoped that it would gradually wear out as I walked. I took out my jacket out o kit bag, and smoothed it down as best I could. I patted the other jacket, which already had wings sewn on along with brand new Sergeant's stripes.

Tim came back eventually with his uniform. The buttons were black, they had not been cleaned since he left Manchester, and the sea journey had done nothing to improve the lustre.

"And you're an officer!" I said, "Somebody slipped up there."

Tim didn't answer, but took out a huge tin of Brasso and set to work. He was still polishing when I arrived back from breakfast. It was obvious that he would never have them clean in time. "You'll have to borrow one," I said.

Without speaking he jumped up, left the billet, and returned very disconsolately some twenty minutes later. I felt very spruce in my neatly pressed uniform and shining shoes.

"Not a uniform on the camp that isn't being used," Tim screamed. "I told you not to go celebrating last night," I began smugly. "Belt up; you'd have been with us if you hadn't been too busy sneezing." "I feel hellish this morning," I said, remembering my cold. "I couldn't care less about you right now Noble. What the hell am I going to wear?" "Wear your combies," I suggested, but I could see that he was thinking of the other uniform of mine, the one that I had spent a long laborious night sewing on stripes and wings on until my fingers bled.

"Why did you have to get commissioned?" I said, pulling the jacket from my kitbag, "If you hadn't been commissioned you'd have another pair of blues, you know."

"I wish I had never handed the other in now. I should have wangled it," he said, watching me. As soon as I had safely ripped off one set of chevrons he protested mildly, but I flung my jacket at him. "Take it," I said savagely, "and you can re-sew all that back on before you leave tonight."

He caught the jacket, and began pulling bits of thread away. "Hey, it's got the moth in," Tim suddenly shouted. I spun round, and saw he was grinning. Then he caught sight of my trousers. "You're not wearing those, are you?" He asked, looking down, "they're waffled." The mesh marks did not seem to be leaving them, and I began to doubt if they would. But there was nothing else to do; my others were far too creased.

Tim polished furiously, and soon he began to look presentable. Then I heard another anguished cry from him. "No stud!" We began a frantic search for his collar stud, could find none, and I loaned his a cuff link. It was an expandable type, and he swore that every time he breathed the collar wings opened.

Then his shoe lace broke, and was too short to mend. He laced his shoes one eyelet further down, and let down his trousers a little.

We could hear frantic shouts and scurrying outside and knew that parade time was very near. Tim rushed round in an all-out effort to be finished on time, and when we heard the flight leader calling our names we rushed out, Tim pulling on his jacket and doing it up on the way. It fitted him badly, and the top button looked as though it would burst at any time. "It'll probably shoot off and hit the guy in the eye just as he's pinning on my wings," Tim grinned. "You've had your commission, then, you know," I said.

We went to the armoury and drew rifles, feeling very conspicuous and proud in front of the chaps on later courses, who were drawing their rifles. All the courses were on the Wings parade, and there was no flying or lectures that day.

We longed around waiting for the signal from the officers. Our flight commander came and gave us a pep talk on the 'smarten up' lines. I think he despaired of our rifle drill, and he had vainly gone through all the movements with us in the evenings. We were still fairly shoddy, but he was hoping for the best.

I had arranged to go to Johannesburg for leave. Tim was going to Pretoria to attend his commissioning details, and naturally the talk was full of the things we were going to do on leave. Although he was pleased about his commission Tim felt a little out of it, for all his immediate friends were sergeants. Alan Afton would, of course, be a Second Lieutenant, but Glen Phillips was to be a sergeant again, as was George Marsden. So was Les Forester, whose wife was in the Wrens, and who had recently been commissioned herself. "Just my blasted luck," moaned Les, "I can't face going back to her yet." If ever a man needed an incentive to work hard and get a commission, it was Les.

Taffy, too, poor soulful Taffy was also to be an NCO, but Geoff Barker, the money lender from Yorkshire, was to be commissioned, and in a magnanimous moment on hearing the news he declared that all transactions contracted between certain dates would be cancelled. I was thankful to the powers that be for selecting Geoff to be an officer, for not only did it wipe off a fifteen shilling debt I owed him, but it also got rid of him. Tim was not quite so happy about it, for he and Geoff were the only two to be selected to go on an Instructor's Training course, and they would, for a while, be buddies.

The rest of us, apart from the South Africans, were to be posted as Staff pilots to various parts of the union. The South Africans were posted to Operational Training Units in North Africa. They had our blessing – and our envy.

The band started playing, and the Parade was on. We formed up, slung our rifles, and marched. We marched past a dais erected for the occasion, and a Brigadier who was to present the wings took the salute.

As we neared the dais most of us smartened up quite considerably, for this was the moment we had waited for. This was the moment we had dreamed of, since the day oh so long ago, when we were recruits; boys suddenly thrust into the turmoil of service life. This was the moment I thought would never come, a moment I had lived time and time again. It was the greatest moment of my life. I was about to get my wings, to qualify as an RAF pilot, and whatever happened, no-one could ever take that away from me. From now I would not be in the RAF, I would be an RAF pilot – and there was, and still is, a distinct difference.

We halted on the parade ground, and the band played the Inspection Waltz as the Brigadier, our own Colonel, the CI, the CFI, and our flight commanders walked slowly by us in inspection. I hoped that no one would notice my trousers. Tim must surely be holding his breath, I thought.

The Inspection was over, and we heaved quiet sighs of relief. The wags started mouthing their indiscretions as the officers walked out of earshot. I waggled my toes, for I had read that the guards did that when standing to attention for a long time.

We were ordered to stand at ease, and the presentation began. The leading pupil, the one who had received the highest marks for ground work and flying was called out, and received a cup and congratulations from the Brigadier. He was a South African, later to receive many distinctions in the desert. Then alphabetically we were called out to receive out wings.

I waited with apprehension for my name to be called. There it was, I heard it. It seemed muffled and far away. I knew the drill, had practised it, and did exactly as I should. It is very rare that anyone boobs on a wings parade. The Brigadier shook my hand, and as he pinned the wings on my jacket he said a few words, shook my hand again, and I returned to my place in the rank. That was it, it was all over.

We waited for other pupils to receive their wings, and then after a few words from the Brigadier and the Colonel we were marched away from the parade ground and were quickly dismissed.

Wings Parade was over. The relief was tremendous, and everyone was hail fellow well met. We slapped each other on the back, had a quick smoke, and then drifted back in groups to the mess.

I looked in the mail pigeon holes. Most of them were stacked with telegrams and there were one or two letters. I fished my little pile out. Amongst the telegrams was one letter, dated a month previous. It was the letter that Tim had long ago prophesied I would get one day. The 'goodbye' letter.

But I didn't mind at all. I had my Wings, and I had some telegrams to open.

Chapter 14

As the train pulled into the small station on the outskirts of Johannesburg, Frank waved from the window at our hosts. I had some misgivings at meeting them, for whereas Frank knew the family well – they were actually related to the girl he was engaged to in Axminster – I had never met them, and I felt like an intruder.

But I should not have worried. Mrs. Cooke clamped me to her very ample self as though she had know me all my life, Mr. Cooke wrung my hand, and said that I looked thirsty, and Margaret, nine, and coquettish deposited a resounding kiss on my cheek, and from then on I was a member of the family.

Their ancient car rattled us to their home in an avenue about a mile from the town, and Frank and I were plumped ceremoniously on the veranda. "What did the Governor of North Carolina say to the Governor of South Carolina, Frank?" asked Mr. Cooke, a twinkle in his eye.

Frank was prepared for this. "It's a long time between drinks, I think, " said Frank, giving me a wink, at which Mr. Cooke broke out into uncontrollable laughter, as he ambled off to fetch a bottle. Margaret flew out with some table tennis bats, and tried to organise a game of ping pong. Mrs. Cooke put on some records, and sang to them in a high contralto voice, unfortunately not synchronised with the music. The little black skinned servant that the Cooke's had came to the door, stared at us, and grinned, and when we grinned back she became as shy as a schoolgirl, and made a hasty retreat to the kitchen. Now and again as someone came up the road they would stop, and shout, "So your visitors are here?" to which Mrs. Cooke would come out to the step, stand arms akimbo, and laughingly suggest that if they had any suggestions for adding to our entertainment, they should not be shy to come forward. Every person who stopped invited us, either to their home, or for a drive, or a drink, or a show or party. "Can't have you lads lonely, can we?" said Mrs. Cooke.

Mr. Cooke was not long before he appeared with the brandy and ginger, chuckling that this was the earliest sundowner that he had ever had. The little servant girl brought a tray of salted nuts, and Margaret brought some fruit and sat on my knee.

Most of the people who lived round the Cooke's were employed in the gold mines, we learned. Mr. Cooke, himself a mines detective, promised that he would arrange a trip round a mine if we wished. Mrs. Cooke was a Commandant of the Red Cross, and Margaret a junior member, and it wasn't long before we were proudly shown their uniforms.

I felt the brandy going to my head, for I wasn't used to drinking in the daytime, but each time my glass was empty it was miraculously filled up before I would notice. Frank was faring no better than I was, and I felt that we were both becoming a little incoherent. His voice seemed far away, and what he said didn't make sense.

But before things became too bad a meal was served, with Mrs. Cooke sitting at the head of the table, her eyes shining, her large body shaking with laughter, as though she was enjoying every moment. Mr. Cooke carved up two chickens with remarkable agility, and Margaret put some records on. I had been in the house for two or three hours and there had not been one complete minute of quiet during the whole of that time. I wondered if it was like that all the time. Frank assured me it was. "These people," he said, waving a fork round the table, "these people live every minute. Wait until they liven up. They're probably a bit shy of you."

At this there was a whoop of delight from Mrs. Cooke, and she dropped the potatoes that she was serving, whilst her body convulsed with laughter. It was absolutely contagious. We were all laughing, and did not know why, but I have seldom enjoyed a meal or such company, wearing though it was.

After dinner we calmed down a little, drank coffee and liqueurs, and smoked ourselves into a wonderful state of drowsiness in the easy chairs on the stoop outside.

The evening drew in a little, and the air became cooler. Lights were switched on, and their glow on the heaps of gorgeous flowers and shrubs that abundantly filled the little gardens of the houses in the avenue was like something in Technicolor. The scents from these plants wafted down the avenue in invisible waves, and I wanted to sit there forever.

But suddenly there was a screech of brakes, a car stopped, and a man in evening clothes appeared. He was introduced to us as Dan, and had come, it seemed, to take us a Bobby Burns night at the Caledonian Club. "A surprise for you," laughed Mrs. Cooke, "and as long as you're back by morning, we shan't come looking for you."

Mr Cooke was busy asking Dan what the Governors said to each other, and Frank and I escaped into the bedroom to smarten up a bit.

The bedroom window was wide open, and as we were changing, I sensed that somebody was there; I saw something moving. Before I could investigate a horse pushed its head through. "I can see," I remarked, "that one has to be prepared for anything in this house." "That'll be Firefly," said Frank, "she belongs to Margaret."

I looked through the window, and could see Margaret in the garden, which was rapidly becoming darker. She saw me and came over. "It's her bedtime," she explained. "She always sleeps in the front garden." "Won't she run away?" I asked. "She often does," said the little girl, "and daddy has to get the car out and look for her. Most people round here know her now, and if they see her they catch her and keep her until the morning." "What happens if she doesn't stray to a friend?" I asked.

"Oh, we have to go to the pound for her then. She'll end up there alright, if nobody catches her. Trouble is, though, that when she goes there, daddy has to pay to get her out, and then he gets cross. She is a bit of a nuisance," she went on, and then nuzzled her face into the horse, "but I love her. Oh, I love her."

She pulled Firefly away from the window, and let her towards the garden. "You know," she said, upon her return, "when she knows you a bit better, you can ride her." And then, very confidentially, she added, "I'll show you how to make her gallop, but don't tell mummy I showed you."

I had never been on a horse in my life, but I looked forward to a ride on Firefly. "You'll regret it," said Frank, who had been listening. "Why?" I asked. "The horse looks meek enough, and she is only a pony."

"It's alright Margaret saying she'll show you how to make him gallop. What she can't show you is how to make him stop. I rode him once. She ran off with me, I couldn't do a thing with her, and she rode me all through town causing absolute havoc in the main street. Eventually a policeman stopped her, and I had to calm the animal down, and lead her back here. Mrs Cooke nearly had hysterics when she was me."

"That I can well imagine," I said. "I've never met a woman who can laugh so much." "They're good types," said Frank, simply.

It was quite dark when we climbed into Dan's car. The Cooke's waved us off, after we declined one for the road. Dan kept up a running commentary all the way to the club. He showed us the mine where he was manager; reeled off the names of all the people that he expected would be at club, and told us what he expected would happen.

"Wait until they bring in the haggis," laughed Dan, "that's when the fun really starts." "I suppose everybody there will be a Scot, or of a Scot descent?" I asked. "A lot of them are, of course, but there'll be a lot of outsiders like ourselves," he explained, "by special invitation, and various ways and means."

We went first into the bar, which was built on the lines of an American cocktail bar, and which, even though it was quite early, was crowded. We sat down at the bar, and Dan introduced us to many of his friends. He seemed to know everybody, and my head reeled trying to keep not of the many names. But, so far, there was no Mac, nor a name that even suggested the Highlands of Scotland. There were, however, quite a number of men in kilts, and one or two ladies wore a sash of tartan material. Everyone else was in evening dress, and Frank and I seemed to be conspicuous in our uniforms.

More people drifted into the bar, and we were introduced. Still no Macs. Dan was plying us with drinks faster than we could drink them, and I felt a little weary after the afternoon's bout. But the general gaiety and high spirits of everyone soon lulled me into false security, and I noticed that Frank was doing exceedingly well in keeping up with Dan. The noise became louder, more people came in, and everyone was in a party mood.

And then we met our first real Scotsman. He wore a kilt, had a rugged look, as though he had just been plucked from glens, and I swear I could smell the heather on him. Moreover his name was MacDonald. Dan introduced us, and MacDonald said, "You must pardon me, I speak very little English," in a curious accent that I could not define. "Mac," said Dan, "is from Brittany, and speaks French. He is the only French Scotsman I know."

Mac stayed with us. He was a morose individual, intent on getting quite drunk. "You see," he explained, "when I am drunk I speak the Scottish very good. You see? I improve on one drink." He downed another, and went on, "And on two, Bettair – and on three," he downed another, "bettair still."

I asked how much he needed to make him speak perfectly. He grinned slyly. "Oodles," he said, and the improvement was remarkable.

After we had been in the bar over an hour Dan suggested that we went to our tables. Good idea, I thought. The tables were set out in rows, arranged round a small polished piece of floor for dancing. A few couples were already there dancing to a melodious little band. We settled ourselves at the table, and almost immediately a waiter came over, and Dan ordered more drinks. "Might as well make a night of it, boys," he said.

Frank and I had had enough, and we left our drinks untouched. Frank got up to dance, and very soon I saw him whirling around the small floor; my feet too began to itch, and I spied a girl sitting moderately unattached on the far side of the room. I made my way across, and the girl greeted me, smilingly. She was a slender pretty girl, dressed in a flowing blue frock which billowed as she danced. Me feet, clumsy at the best of times when dancing were tonight like a couple of heavy bricks, but the girl, by discreet pressure guided us both round in a passable imitation of the waltz. She didn't exactly say that I danced divinely, but neither did she complain.

"What part of Scotland are you from?" she asked. "That part called England," I replied. She was unimpressed by my devastating wit, and continued, "I'm from Dundee. Have you ever been?" I shuddered. "Yes, I've been to Dundee. I spent a night there, I remember." "I came here before the war," went on the girl, "but I still have folks in Dundee. I have an Uncle there – he's a policeman." "I know a policeman in Dundee!" I replied. "Does your uncle like crossword puzzles?" "Och, no," said the girl, laughing. "He runs a police station, and has no time for anything like that." I was glad. That would have been stretching co-incidence too far.

I saw the girl back to her table, promising to call on her again later in the evening. But I had no chance of doing so. Frank had persuaded Dan to run us home, and in the car Frank told me quietly that he had discovered that Dan was on the early shift at the mine in the morning, which meant that in a little over four hours he would have to be at work.

When we arrived at the house Mr. Cooke greeted us with the inevitable brandy bottle and asked that same question.

"It's a long time between beds," we said in chorus, "Goodnight." We left Dan and Mr. Cooke sitting in the cool of the stoop sipping their last sundowners of the day.

Chapter 14a

A week or so later Frank and I received a telegram ordering us to report to a small town where there was an Air School, and where we would apparently undergo further training.
We had both been selected as Staff pilots. This selection I understood took the form of a weed out. The best pilots went as instructors, the most fearless went to an operational training unit for eventual operations, the clever, cool pilots went to Coastal Command, and the rest went as Staff pilots to various schools in the Union.

Frank and I were to be trained as Navigational pilots, and would soon be posted to a Navigational Training School where we would fly pupil navigators on exercises – a prospect that excited us as much as a snowstorm would an Eskimo.

However, that was our lot, and comparatively degrading though it may have been, someone had to do it, and we kidded ourselves that it was important.

"Anyway," said Frank, "we aren't pupils any more. We should be comfortable there – no early morning parades or crowded billets."

We caught the train in the afternoon, and met up with one or two more contemporaries heading for the same Air School. We commandeered a compartment and the usual school of cards started before we were even out of the station.

I wished that Tim had been with me, but he had been commissioned and posted as an instructor, and I never saw him again. Alan Afton had gone up to the Middle East for immediate operational duties, and George Marsden and his blackbird had been posted as an instructor. Glen Phillips, the wizened little sergeant, had not been commissioned, but had also gone on the instructor's course.

I met up again with Les Forester, whose wife had joined the Wrens, and who was getting ample mail, it seemed, for he was reading a letter when I spotted him. He looked miserable, but he greeted me cheerfully. He had been posted to a different SFTS, but the end of his training, and subsequent posting had co-incited with ours, although he no longer had leave.

"How's the wife?" I asked. "Still in the Wrens?" "Just been commissioned!" Les said. I looked at his sergeant's tapes, new and bright, and understood his misery. "Thank god I wasn't posted home. I couldn't have borne the humiliation."

He put his letter down, and asked "heard anything about this place we're posted to?"
I shook my head. "It should be alright, though. Remember," I said, remembering Frank's words, "we're not pupils any more. We're senior NCOs, and should get some advantages. There won't be much bull."

"Shouldn't be," agreed Forester, "I hope there's a good mess and decent billets." "Bound to be decent billets for senior NCOs," I added.

Frank joined us, and we sat chatting, until the curious notes of the dinner xylophone called us to a meal. We quizzed each other for information about each Air School we were going to, but nobody seemed to know anything about it, other than it was on the coast and was reputed to be a tiny but popular holiday resort.

We ate a wonderful meal of paw paw, soup, fish, which according to the menu was shark; a delicious curry with eggplant, followed by avocado pears, granadillas, tangerines and grapes – a whole mountain of fruit, and for those of us who had room – coffee.

After the meal we sipped cool beer until suddenly it was quite dark, and we all agreed on an early night. When we got back to the compartment we saw that the beds had been made up for us, and we soon slid between the sheets, all of us wondering what the new camp was going to be like.

It was the next evening before we arrived at the tiny station, which we learned was some eight miles from the camp. We bullied Frank into acting as Officer in charge of postings which meant he had to organise transport for us. He went off to the telephone, and as sometimes happens, no transport was available, at least not until later and he was requested to phone again around nine o'clock. This meant we had to hang around for some three hours, so we decided to have a look at the town.

This took us all half an hour, during which time we walked from end to end and side to side. We saw its church, its cinema, its hotel, its taxi and its one coloured lady of easy virtue. We spent the rest of the half hour reading the Strand Magazine in the Toc H before we were apologetically thrown out.

I was glad that we were only spending three weeks here, for it was about the most lifeless place that I had ever seen, but I imagined that we should not be coming into town very often, the camp would have as many amenities as this town. We urged Frank to phone again, which he did, but without any luck. It was almost dark, and we decided that the only thing to do was to have a drink.

The small hotel boasted a nice little bar, and we settled down to our wait. It was empty apart from a Corporal who sat at a table immersed in a newspaper, completely ignoring us.

The beer was quite good, but we weren't in a very merry mood and didn't have much of it. We all wanted to get settled in at the new camp, to sample the sergeants' mess for the first time, to perhaps be assigned our very own private billet, and to be able to send the coloured waiters scurrying around.

We were very much senior NCO conscious – the success of actually getting our wings had perhaps gone to our heads a little, and we were somewhat chagrined to find that there had been no welcoming committee at the station to greet us.

"Wish I was in Bournemouth," said Les Forester. "Is that where the wife is?" I asked him. "Gosh, no, I didn't mean for that. She's in Edinburgh." "I should have thought that's where you wanted to be," said Frank, with one of his innocent, and not very concealed winks. Les looked uncomfortable. "I daren't meet up with her until I'm commissioned," he said. I stared at him. He really meant it. "You're not serious, Les?" I asked. "You don't know my wife." "Any photographs?" I was intrigued.

He delved into his tunic pocket, and pulled out a portrait of his wife. She was strikingly beautiful, dark, with large lustrous eyes, which seemed full of love and life as they looked out calmly from the flatness of the photograph. "She's lovely," I remarked with feeling. "I wish I was in Edinburgh," said Frank, with a serious nod.

Les looked calmly at Frank, but said nothing. I could see that he resented the remark, bantering though it had been. He looked as though he was going to say something, and then quickly changed his mind. "She still write to you every day?" I asked, handing back the photo.

Les hesitated, and his brow furrowed slightly. "No – she's very busy, it seems," and then, as though to dismiss the subject he asked, "anybody for another beer?"

We could see that the matter was closed, and changed the subject. Something was eating Les, he was not nearly as talkative as he had once been, he had the air of a person brooding over something, and I hoped that I was wrong in my guess as to what it was. Frank went off to the phone again, then, so I was left alone with Les. I said nothing for a moment, and then opened the conversation by asking him about the cricket at Johannesburg – he had told me earlier that he been once or twice when on leave.

I thought he was going to answer, but he leaned over, and said a very curious thing. "They tell me that if you can get an Anson into a spin, you can't get out of it."

I looked at him, eager for a clue to his strangeness recently, but Frank shouted from the doorway, "Come on, chaps." We went back to the station, where the rest of the posting was waiting, and soon a lorry arrived, and we were on our way to camp. Les was sitting at the far end, and I couldn't speak to him, so I decided to forget it. Months later I realised why he had made that remark.

We rolled over the dusty roads, and soon saw the twinkling lights of the camp. We left Frank and his brother officers at a brightly lit bungalow next to the officer's mess, and then we drove round to the sergeants' mess, a less imposing building, but brightly lit, with hundreds of moths flitting round the unguarded lamps in the entrance.

A Flight Sergeant greeted us. "Follow me and draw bedding," he said. My heart sank at these words. It was no better than being a pupil. We grumbled and groused, but drew the bedding and blankets, and then, thankfully, sheets. "Where are the billets, Flight?" somebody queried.

The Flight Sergeant pointed to a row of neatly pointed khaki tents. "Over there," he said, "Four men to a tent."

The next morning I woke to find myself covered in the foulest bug bites that I had ever seen. 'Its true then', I thought, 'Bugs do bite Senior NCOs.'

Chapter 15

There is a saying in the Air Force that when even sparrows are grounded the Anson can still fly.

This aircraft, a modest twin-engined affair was primarily built in 1929 as a general reconnaissance machine; it was modified as a bomber, sent to Coastal Command for general duties, and when war broke out comprised the bulk of our bombing power. It was used as a night fighter, on reconnaissance and for photography, for leaflet raids, for dropping torpedoes and depth charges and for carrying VIP's throughout the wartime skies of Britain.

As our bomber strength grew and the Anson became outdated and too slow for operational duties, it carried on its service in Training Command throughout the Commonwealth.

I was introduced to this versatile and robust of all aeroplanes by a South African who had flown everything from Spitfires to Walruses. "The Anson is like a woman," he said, and though we who were gathered round his scoffed like true senior NCOs, he went on, "treat her gently, with respect and forbearance, and she's yours for life." He looked round at us and grinned. "Who wants the first date?" he asked.

I was the only one who had (mistakenly) drawn a parachute, so I was nudged forward.

The South African sat in the left seat and I sat in the co pilots' seat. "One circuit and bump," he said, "Watch, and then you can have a crack."

He signalled to the mechanic to start up, and I watched every manoeuvre. It wasn't very different from the Oxford on which I had been trained, apart from one disturbing fact. The undercarriage had to be wound up by hand. I struggled and turned the handle, which is down by the right of the pilot, and entails contortion of the body for easy manipulation.

I watched the pilot as much as possible, drinking in all the vital actions while he carried on a shouting running commentary on what he was doing. As soon as I had would up the undercarriage it was almost time to wind it down again. Luckily it became fully locked down an instant before we landed, and I leaned back exhausted. The instructor grinned again. "Don't worry about that. When you're flying pupils, that'll be their job." Relieved, I gave him a sickly smile.

We changed places, and I took off on my first circuit and landing. There was no hitch, and this time the instructor wound up the undercarriage. I landed, and he got out and told me to solo. The aircraft handled perfectly, although my airspeed came quite close to stalling speed as I juggled with the undercarriage. However, I completed the landing safely and spent the rest of the morning getting to know my 'date'.

The followed a week of lectures with little flying. Navigation theory was crammed into us, and soon it became apparent that not one of us would ever get lost if we were detailed to fly from Capetown non-stop to Berlin.

On my first night flying trip I became hopelessly and utterly lost when flying only sixty miles from the aerodrome. Frank had been detailed to fly as navigator, and we were to fly a right angled triangle covering approximately two hundred miles.

We gathered out kit and I met Frank at the aircraft with a large green canvas bag which contained all his gear – computers – rules, protractors, and all the paraphernalia necessary for flight by night without a wireless operator.

I climbed to a thousand feet above the airfield and set course on the reading that Frank had calculated from his flight plan. He sat behind me at a little table, and every few minutes he would tap me and hand me a modified course, allowing for changed of wind at various altitudes. He also told me to continue climbing.

After we had completed the first leg he handed me another course to fly. I reset the compass, and turned on to it, set the gyro to the altered course, and settled down in comfort. It was easy. Frank was doing all the work.

Very soon I was surprised to see that we had run into cloud. At the briefing I understood that there was no cloud to be expected on the route, but allowing for the fact that even the met men can be wrong I was not unduly worried until Frank tapped me on the shoulder.

"Cloud," he said. I nodded. "Where's it come from?" he asked blandly. "It just appeared," I said. "Shouldn't be any. What have you been up to?" he asked. "Your fault," I said, "You're the navigator. I'm concentrating on keeping us straight and level. Give me another course. A proper one," I added.

He went indignantly back to his table and in a few moments popped back with a new course. I altered course, and the he tapped me on the shoulder again, and pointed outside, and down. I looked down and could see nothing – no light, only the shimmering of more cloud well below us.

"More cloud," I said. "My foot," said Frank, "that's sea." I looked again, and knew that he was right. This was serious. We had no right to be anywhere near the sea. "Perhaps it's a big lake," I suggested. Frank snorted, very close to my ear. "Yes, probably Lake Zambesi."

He then came closer to me and whispered, "You are a silly little man aren't you?" I grinned. "You're the navigator, I'm the captain. I demand a proper course to get us out of this little mess. Otherwise I'll have you cashiered." He whispered again, and pointed to the compass. "Do you always fly blue on red, captain?" he asked, baring his teeth.

My ears burned as I looked at the compass. It was wrongly set, and I was flying a reciprocal course to the one Frank had given.

He stomped back to his table and in a few moments handed me another memo. I thought it was a change of course, but it was a message, and read: To Captain from Navigator. Respectfully suggest that you are dozy, incompetent and have something on your mind. Have I your permission to bale out?

I looked round. Frank was putting on his parachute. I told him to cut out the fooling and give me a course, but he refused, so I turned on to the reciprocal of the one we had been flying, and informed him by memo. I also wrote: Be a good lad, and I'll help you cook your log.

He did eventually give me a course, adding that as far as he could make out that would bring us near the airfield, and would I please not disturb him as he was looking for the position that we would hit the coast again, and would try and recognise it, again setting a further course from there.

He did find a small town that he thought he recognised when we eventually hit the coast. I asked him could we not follow the coast until we hot our own little holiday resort.

He agreed, and watched the coastline. After a few minutes on this course I saw stretched below us a fine white cloud. At first I was not unduly worried, but after half an hour and the whiteness stretched all around us I was. I realised that by now we should nearing the town. How to find it through the cloud?

I asked Frank to let me know when he thought we would be over the town. "Are you kidding Noble?" he sneered. "You've mucked me up something shocking. I haven't a clue."

I began losing height, and immediately he scurried to his table. He handed me a memo with an estimated time of arrival. "Not accurate," he shouted, "What are you going to do?" "Keep the same airspeed," I answered, "turn out to sea, losing height, and break through the cloud at that exact time you've written down there."

He shrugged, and probably realised as well as I did that it was the right thing to do. Evidently the cloud had clamped in unexpectedly, and certainly covered the airfield which we were pretty sure was in the vicinity.

I lost height down to 1,500 feet, and we were then flying just on top of the cloud. I had turned slightly out to sea, and hoped that I had turned enough. I did not like the idea of breaking through low cloud over land, for although it was fairly flat around the airfield there was one or two small mountains and some high ground on the coastline.

On Frank's estimated time I dived through the cloud. I could feel Frank's tense clutching on my seat, and my hands were sweating. A thousand feet, and we were still in cloud.

The altimeter showed 500 feet before we finally broke. The sea seemed almost on top of us, grey and rough, and I heard a cry from Frank. Instinctively I pulled up the nose, and turned. "I thought we'd had it," he shouted. "Now get us back, bright boy."

I turned the aircraft until we could see lights and I flew low towards them. "Try and pick a pinpoint," I said to Frank.

It was easy. As we came nearer to the light we both recognised a weak searchlight that the Aircraft Controller pointed straight into the sky for such occasions. Frank patted my back, and I felt that I had somewhat redeemed myself. But I didn't feel so good when, after landing, Frank tumbled out of the aircraft and kissed the ground.

Chapter 16

The course, though slow, was gruelling and seemed cruelly slow. We were all glad to leave the Air School where we had converted to Ansons, and had become, during the process, fully fledged Staff Pilots.

Once again we were in a train bound for another part of the Union, and once again we knew little of the camp or the town to which we had been posted – although there had been the usual chorus of wails by some who professed to be in the know. "It's in the back of beyond, "said one, and another, "regular glasshouse of a place. Bags of bull, etc."

However when the train arrived, and we were collected from the station by lorry promptly and efficiently, it certainly seemed better organised than our last port of call.

From the back of the lorry I glimpsed a modern cinema; a few busy shops, many modern cars, and a café. Then we turned from the town into a long narrow road, and in a few moments we were in the camp – another Air School.

We were put down at the Sergeants' Mess, and allocated billets – real ones this time, not tents. I was dismayed to find each leg of my bed standing in a small can of paraffin. This denoted the presence of the pestilential bug again. But there were clean sheets and once can't have everything.

"What a dump," said Bill Trippett, tall and suave, and reckoned to be the intellectual of the group. He heaved his luggage – his was essentially luggage, ours was kit – onto his bed, and proceeded to unpack. I had not known Bill very long, and wasn't particularly keen on being billeted with him, for he had a chip on his shoulder over his not being offered a commission. He was droll, slow moving, caring not one jot for authority. He was a number one man. "Number one, first," he often said. He also always carried a book with him – a good book, of course. At that moment he was carrying Richard Hillary's Thin Blue Line around with him. I think he would have been a second Richard Hillary if fate had not decreed that he be a staff pilot, and an uncommissioned one at that.

Next to my bed a pilot with a shock of blond hair hanging neatly over his eyes offered a pack of cigarettes around. I was annoyed that he had taken this bed – I was trying to save it for Kenny Lambert who had shared a tent with me. However I took one of his cigarettes. I looked at his kitbag for his name. J. Brown, it had scrawled across it in large black letters. First name is bound to be John, I guessed.

He knew Kenny quite well, I gathered from the mutual tumultuous welcome they gave each other. I stood to one side feeling piqued. Why was It, I wondered, that other people's friends were always meeting up with each other, and I always seemed to be saying goodbye to mine, and never seeing them again. Even Frank had gone, being posted to another Air

School. I started counting up the people I had known, and hot not seen again, but it proved a little boring so I gave it up, and asked them both to come across to the mess.

"How did you know my name? J. Brown asked. I looked at him, exaggerating surprise. "Perhaps it's the way your soul goes marching on," I eventually answered, when I saw he really was waiting for a reply. He groaned. "Crikey," he muttered, "I've been getting that crack since I weaned," and from then on we were the best of pals.

There was, indeed, a motley crowd in the Sergeants' Mess. I looked round carefully as I went in, as this was the first Mess that I had been in that was not either a pupils or a Transit Camp. It was permanent, and I hoped it would seem different.

South African sergeants, Staff sergeants and one sergeant major mixed with RAF sergeants, flight sergeants, and Warrant Officers, with a couple of WAAF sergeants sitting quietly by themselves crocheting and quaffing huge glasses of beer.

All looked us carefully up and down, some with obvious dislike; others with subdued interest. The WAAF sergeants smirked into their beer. The look on their faces suggested that they hoped there was better to come.

We bought some drinks and stood to one side of the bar. Immediately Johnny stated talking to the most senior member he could see, an RAF Warrant Officer, Wireless Operator/Air Gunner, who, it appeared, was having a rest from operations in the Middle East, and had been at the Air School only a few weeks.

It was then we heard for the first time the curious clipped mixture of English, Arabic and Kaffir slang that we were to hear for the rest of our stay there, brought down from the Middle East by these ex-operational types.

Picking some of the more repeatable sentences out, the conversation went something like this:-
"What the food like?"
"Monjary? Grim! Baas!" The last word, now and on the frequent occasions when it was used subsequently was delivered with the chin jutting firmly out, and the head tossed into the air.
"Get much flying in?"
"First diddle, second diddle, three times a week. Baas! Grim!"
I could see Johnny was dying to ask what a diddle was, but I hoped he wouldn't. The Air Gunner went on,
"Been short of Peeloes till you bods came. No Peeloes. Baas!"
"What's the town like?"
"Definite grim."
"What's the beer like?"
"Definite grim."

"You like it here?"

"Definite grim," he added, "see you bahdin." He walked away chanting "Orrangies, laamonahd, aigs-a-braid, Johnny!"

Kenny laughed, "So that's what the desert does to you. Thank god I was posted here."

We chatted with one or two of the characters standing round the bar, and found out many things that we wanted to know – the run of the camp, the moods of the CO, what was expected of us regarding ground duties and pickets, bar prices, meal times, the arrangements for Air Sea Rescue, the weather we could expect, what to wear and when to wear it, but unfortunately, as there were no pilots in the mess we could learn nothing about the actual flying duties. We assumed that every other pilot on the station must be commissioned or teetotal.

Presently more pilots who had arrived with us found their way to the mess, considerably consolidating our position there, which was noticeable by increasing friendliness from those who, until now, had stood eyeing us without venturing to speak.

We went into the meal feeling as though we were at last permanent members of an Air Station, still a training school perhaps, but we were no longer pupils.

During the meal we were joined by more wireless operator air gunners, mostly flight sergeants or warrant officers, and all of them battle-hardened, impervious to mess etiquette or dress regulations, now resting from operations. They began by telling our hungry heads of flying conditions at the school, all of them talking at once, gesticulating wildly, but the conversation soon drifted into line shooting of the strongest kind – after all we were very green pilots, and none of us had any knowledge of either the Middle East or of operational flying.

But we nodded our heads and clicked our tongues in the right places, and by the end of the meal they had taken us to their hearts. I knew this because during the middle of the sweet one of them held out his cigarettes to Johnny and said, "Have a cigarette, skip."

We all sat in the mess long after the tables had cleared away. I was rather surprised that the wireless operators had not gone into the bar where the general hubbub of voices now drowned even our loud conversation.

I turned to a warrant officer, and asked him if he were perhaps night flying. "First and second diddle. And me with a date in town. Definite poor show."

He went on to tell me that they usually flew a three hour detail, landed, had a cup of tea and then set off for another three hours. When they landed again at about 3 a.m. they had a meal and went to bed. Sometimes they were on a late afternoon detail the following day, but more often it was night flying the following night. It was the same for pilots, so I imagined that I would soon be putting up some hours in the log book.

The warrant officer got up from the table, "Come on you lot," he said, "this isn't the desert." A flight sergeant opposite demurred, "it isn't time, yet."

The warrant officer pointed to the hands on his watch, "What's that, fog?" he asked. They all rose with much chair scraping, and trooped out of the mess bored at the prospect of a first and second diddle when they could be on a date in town.

Johnny, Ken and I went back to our billet, one of a three roomed hut, with a veranda. We found Bill Trippett sitting on the veranda, reading by the light leaking from the window.

"Have you seen the orders, you lot?" he asked. We hadn't – we had walked by them in the entrance to the mess, but on his advice we went back to have a look.

I found that I was due for a flight check in the morning, a navigational detail as second pilot in the afternoon, and circuit and landings, followed by a check at night. The other two were the same. "No wasted time here." I said. Johnny shook his head. "Definite grim," he said. Ken threw back his head, jutted his chin, and added, "Baas!"

Chapter 17

Our next few days at the Air School were taken up with sorting ourselves out, settling in, being accepted by the members of the mess, gaining the respect of the pupil navigators, who knew, of course, just how green we were. This transition from pupil to working pilot could not be hurried; it had to come naturally, and in its own time.

We met the CO who flew his own Harvard, and had holes in his socks; we met the Officer in charge of Air Sea Rescue, and we were terribly disappointed when we found out that he too had just got his wings, and that his sole qualifications for Air Sea Rescue work was a tour on Sunderland Flying Boats as Air Gunner. We met, too, the NCO in charge of pigeons, a bespectacled man with a crew cut who spoke with a lisp when addressing us, but for some unfathomable reason, never when he spoke to his birds, which was more often anyway; and we met the then officer in charge of Flying who had a little Fiat car, circumferenced by a painted white dotted line with the words, "To open, cut along the dotted line" stencilled on the doors.

We met the WAAF in charge of parachutes, who mournfully doled them out, saying "Sign here. Five bob fine if you open them accidentally. This is for flowers for those that don't open in emergency." Nobody asked how the fund stood.

And we met the senior pilot in the Sergeant's Mess – a Warrant Officer who had been flying and drinking since the beginning of time and who looked as though he had hated every minute. When he wasn't flying and he wasn't drinking he listened to a recording of the melancholy Air on a G String, playing it over and over again in the solitude of his billet.

By far the strangest man we met, however, was a tiny South African, a Staff sergeant fitter. He was regarded with awe, horror and disbelief for he was a hypnotist, and never reluctant to display his unusual gifts.

The first time that I saw him in action was in the mess anteroom. Johnny and I had gone for a drink, found the mess deserted, and hearing some sort of commotion in the anteroom we peered in. A group of people surrounded the Staff sergeant, who was speaking to someone who was sitting on a chair. I asked if they had fainted, but was told by a dozen voices to hush, somebody was under the influence.

I watched, fascinated, as the little man spoke quietly to his victim. There was no waving of hands, no dramatic staring from the eyes, just the gentle voice, explaining as one would do to a child that he was getting a little sleepy.

I looked at the man in the chair. He was sitting relaxed and looked comfortable. There was a little smile on his lips that suggested he wasn't taking the thing too seriously. The staff sergeant evidently thought so too, for he admonished the man, very gently, very quietly, with no sound of anger in his voice. "You must give your will completely to me," he was saying, "if you don't I cannot force you. Relax yourself – think only of what I am saying. If you don't want to give your will, if you don't want to think only of what I am saying you are wasting my time, and what's worse, your own."

The droning voice went on similarly for some minutes, and then somebody whispered, "He's under." The relaxed body on the chair was indeed under, and the hypnotist then asked him to get up and walk slowly to the mess anteroom, and to look for his brother. The man walked slowly round, peering at the faces of the bystanders who found it difficult to repress their giggles. Each time he stopped, the Staff sergeant said, "No, that's not your brother – look further." And the man passed on.

He looked at me, and thankfully passed on. Johnny was not so lucky. "There, I think, is your brother. Now, greet him." The man grinned, gold hold of Johnny's hand, and pumped it, grinning wildly and pinching Johnny's cheeks holding his shoulders and other showings of brotherly affection.

Johnny grinned back. "Ask your brother to come and meet me," said the tiny man. The man asked Johnny to come and meet his friend. Johnny said no thank you, but the man was adamant, and grasped his arm firmly, and though Johnny struggled a little he was piloted over to the hypnotist. I saw Johnny nod his head, and the hypnotist indicated the chair. He spoke quietly to him for a few moments, and I watched Johnny relax himself, close his eyes, and waited to do the bidding of the hypnotist.

He spoke to him again, quietly, talking to him as we had heard him talk to the other man, and suddenly, in no time at all, it seemed, the staff sergeant was saying, "you will now do as I ask you, but first say goodbye to your brother." Johnny got up, walked to his 'brother' and held out his hand. The other man took it, grasped it firmly. Their faces became quite serious as they said goodbye. The hypnotist then snapped his fingers, and Johnny's brother came out of the trance, looked quickly round him for a moment or two, and grinned. "What did you make me do?" he asked innocently. "Nothing much," answered the hypnotist. "I wasn't sure of you. Watch this chap – a perfect subject if there ever was one."

He turned to Johnny again, as there was a murmur from the onlookers all wanting to know how the man who had been under hypnosis had felt. However they all quietened as we heard the staff sergeant instructing Johnny. "You've flown 300 hours on Spitfires," he said, "Now I want you to do a circuit and landing in a brand new Spit. You're all strapped in and ready to go. You've got her, I'm taking the chocks away – taxi out to take off position – do a cockpit check, and take off."

Johnny nodded, and adjusted his imaginary helmet that seemed too tight.

I was amazed as I stood there watching him. As he taxied, using left throttle, instead of the right that he was used to, he moved his head from side to side, over the nose of the aircraft that wasn't there.

At a point he stopped, and we saw him checking instruments, doing a full cockpit check of a spitfire, run up the engine, turn into wind, push his throttle fully open, pulling back slowly on the stick, a quick flick to a lever, a touch here and there to other instruments and levers, and a gentle pull back on the stick. It was amazing – this from a pilot whom I'm sure had never even seen the inside of a Spitfire cockpit, quite different, heavens knows from an Anson cockpit, and quite a different take off procedure, and yet he did it with all the ease and apparent confidence of a veteran.

I watched him fly the imaginary aircraft round the circuit doing things now and again which baffled me, and yet seemed to him so natural and necessary. He flew in and did a landing, taxied in carefully, switched off, and took off his imaginary helmet.

Almost immediately the hypnotist told Johnny quietly that it was very warm, and he would find a comfortable place for him to rest. Johnny wiped his brow, and undid his bush jacket a little. The little staff sergeant then suggested that as there was nobody about he might take off his clothes and do a little sun bathing. I feared that the staff sergeant was going too far – there were a few WAAFs present, and after all, the mess was the mess.

However I need not have worried, for Johnny took his clothes off – but in mime! Then he stood apparently naked, his arms up stretched towards the sun, one arm crooked a little allowing him to shield the strong sun from his eyes. The staff sergeant was talking to him all the time, describing the beauty of the place he was supposed to be in, when without changing the pitch of his voice he exclaimed quickly, "Look out, there are two ladies coming." I have never seen Johnny move so quickly. He reached for his clothes. "They're gone" snapped the staff sergeant, whereupon Johnny, quick as a flash, covered his nakedness as best he could with his hands and arms, bending himself double in the process. At the same time he awoke, and was most surprised, and a tiny bit embarrassed at the position he was assuming. However he grinned, and shook his fist at the staff sergeant, who patted him on the back and thanked him for being a sport.

Johnny said he was going back to the mess after hearing what he had done under the influence. "I'll never live it down," he said.

Bill Trippett was lying on the bed when we got back. He had a glass of beer in his hand and the inevitable book in the other. He listened patiently as Johnny related anything he could remember, adding that he could certainly have resisted being hypnotised.

"You couldn't, you know," said Bill dryly. "No?" "No," went on Bill, a little superciliously, I thought. "I happen to know a good deal about hypnotism." "So do I, as it happens," said Johnny acidly. "I studied Yogi before I joined up." Bill smiled disdainfully. "You did?" He looked down his nose contemptuously. "Tell you what, Bill – I have some knowledge of Yogi, and I could hypnotise you. But only if you didn't resist me."

Bill pooh poohed the idea at first, but Kenny, who had just come in, egged him on. "Go on, have a bash." "Alright," said Bill. "Do your worst."

Johnny asked him to follow him carefully. "I want you to lie down on the floor," he said.

Bill hesitated for a moment, then put down his glass of beer and book and heaved himself off the bed. He lay down on the floor. "Like this?" he asked. Johnny nodded. "Now put your hands under your head. Close your eyes, and start counting slowly." "One, two, three..." "Now I'm going to raise your right foot," said Johnny, "Keep your leg stiff, and carry on counting."

He bent down, and took Bill's foot in his hand, and raised his leg. "Twelve, thirteen..." "Are you warm?" asked Johnny. Not unnaturally Bill answered that he was, for of course it was a warm day. "Then cool off a bit," said Johnny as Kenny poured the remainder of Bill's beer accurately down the trousers of his raised leg.

My horrified eyes travelled from Kenny to Johnny to Bill. To his eternal credit he hadn't battered an eyelid, and it rather an anticlimax, when he said, peeling off his soggy trousers, "That settles it – now I'll have to take a shower."

Flying conditions at the school were almost ideal. The weather, which at that time in training command was the main consideration was usually good – most days were wonderfully clear, eternally blue skies, now and again a whispering breeze, and very rarely cloud of more than four tenths.

Because of this visibility being always first class, and on the few occasions that cloud did come rolling down from the mountains it came in quickly after building up during the day, enabling night flying to be cancelled if it were considered a hazard, or at least an early recall if the aircraft had already taken off.

If cloud appeared from nowhere, however, and the met men had had no warning, night flying could indeed be a little ticklish, for the airfield was in a valley, fairly narrow, with mountains rising to 7,000 feet on either side.

Night flying for the pilots who had no girl friends in town was always popular; there was little else to do apart from the cinema or cafes or hotels outside the camp, and similar on a smaller scale inside the camp.

But there were two duties that were unpopular with all pilots; one was Tarmac Master, which consisted of doing absolutely nothing but wandering around the tarmac where the aircraft were parked, on a rickety yellow bicycle. The other duty, different and worse that being the Tarmac Master was that of Airfield Control Pilot, which functioned only at night.

He had to lay out the flare path, control the aircraft taking off and landing, and when the last aircraft was in he had to collect up the flare path again. The airfield had no runway, no shelter, and o grass, and consequently at times the dust at take off time especially was choking each and every ACP. Each time they would appear in the mess with a film of red dust covering them.

It was my turn for ACP and I wasn't feeling too happy about it, for among other things it meant an early meal alone in the mess, and nothing but a long stint in the dark on a hot dusty airfield.

The Italian waiter served me some soup.

"Zoup, zergeanta." He said. "Ver' hot. You ACP?" I nodded. He nodded his blue close cropped head in sympathy.

"Italia Air Force – no ACP," he said, flashing a huge row of white teeth, and spreading out his arms. He flicked the table with a napkin, and said,

"You join Italia Air Force, zergeanta!" as he made smartly for the kitchen door.

When he came back with the second course he again opened with his verbal sabotage. "You take the flare path in once or twice tonight, zergeanta?" he asked seriously.

For a moment I wondered what he meant, until I remembered that on my last ACP duty I had checked all the aircraft in, doused the flares, and taken in the flare path, loaded all the gear into the lorry and was riding back to the Mess when I heard the drone of an aircraft, and in a dreadful sweat, turned the lorry back. I saw the aircraft join the circuit on the up-wind leg which gave me a few minutes to relay the flare path.

I presumed that I had miscounted or check in the aircraft wrongly, and feared that if the Officer I/C flying heard of it I should be for the proverbial dressing down. How the hell could I have done it, I wondered, as I shouted to the duty crew to get a move on. "And lay the blasted thing straight," I yelled, for I had had complaints that night that it like a switchback from the air.

I cursed as I tried to re-connect the field telephone system, and I prayed that the pilots was one of my friends, otherwise I would never hear the last of it. I saw one or two of the goose necks burst into yellowish fire, and with a quick glance at the aircraft I realised that with the speed they were working the crew would at least have that down in time. I sent the driver off with the jeep to tackle someone discreetly in the wireless office, find out who it was, and if it was a sergeant instructor to tell him to go round again.

I worked feverishly at the Glide Path indicator, a little box which the pilot regulates his rate of descent visually by means of coloured lights as he comes in for the landing. I had to guess the setting, and hoped for the best. The aircraft was now on the downwind leg and signalling his call sign with his bottom fuselage light.

I checked his call sign with the landing list and couldn't see it. Thank heavens, I thought, it doesn't really look as though it was my fault. The jeep came rushing back.

"The clot's not one of ours," said the driver as he jumped out. "What?" I said. "He's from another Air School, about sixty miles away. They're on the R/T telling him where he is." "Is he lost?" I asked. "No, just having a look around," he replied. "He's quite happy, and has apologised for having us lay out the flare path again."

I picked up an Aldis lamp, and signalled 'Go home, dimwit.' As though suddenly taking umbrage, the aircraft heeled over and headed straight for his Air School. We began to take in the flare path again. On the way back to the Mess I asked the driver of the jeep if he knew who the pilot was.

"Some Wing Commander," he said. I laughed. It hadn't turned out to be a bad night after all.

As I sat in the mess recalling this and seeing the grinning Italian also remembering I wondered how he knew about it. I asked him. "On my secret radio," he said. I realised, of course, that if he had a radio he could tune into the frequency we were using, and listen to night flying all night, and I felt sure that it must be bad for security. But nobody cared. I couldn't imagine Mussolini being very interested.

"I'll see the sergeant SP," I said to the Italian, "and have it confiscated." He flicked his duster again, and smiled. "He gave it to me, zergeanta! Good nighta!"

The jeep was waiting for me outside the door of the Mess, and I climbed in. We rounded up the duty crew, who climbed aboard with mugs of tea, and chunky sandwiches in their hands. A little airman handed me a mug. "Plenty more laid on for later, Sergeant," he said.

We made our way across the airfield, and I checked the wind direction in order to find the longest run I could give the aircraft. I pointed in the direction of the flare path. "For gods' sake, get it straight."

The men got to work, and I tested the field telephone, the Glide Path Indicator, and the floodlight. I kept an eye on the men who were lining the flares. It seemed straight enough, and I signalled them to light the wicks. Soon an aircraft taxied out to do a circuit and landing test.

He took off and landed, and signalled that it was satisfactory, and then for half an hour or so we had nothing to do. Darkness was falling quickly, and we stood round the floodlight idly killing beetles or moths attracted to the light.

Soon the first aircraft taxied out. I shone the Aldis lamp on each pilot of a second or two, in order that I may recognise them, and that I may take evasive action from those that I knew would brake hard just after levelling up on the flare path, and who would open up their throttles deliberately showering us in the filthy dust. I knew there were four to watch for: Johnny, Ken, Bill and Tom who had just finished a tour as Tarmac Master after being grounded for six weeks for colliding in mid-air during formation flying practise. I knew that he would be the worst offender of them all.

Each time I recognised them I yelled "Backs!" and we would all turn away covering our faces and ears as best we could. Even though the dust got everywhere, I was still glad to turn away before they took off.

When everyone had gone we had nothing to do for two hours until the first aircraft came in again. The airmen went over to their NAAFI for some tea, which was welcoming, and apart from one flare blowing out, everything was still and quiet.

I checked the aircraft in again, shouting for the floodlight as each aeroplane neared the touch down. Two aircraft were obviously undershooting – I had to flash them a quick red and they went round again.

Soon everyone was down – the navigating pupils would change for others who had been waiting in the crew rooms, and the crews would go to the messes for a quick cup of tea or coffee, whilst the aircraft were refuelled.

We took advantage of the time that no aircraft were in the air to refill the flares with paraffin, and once again we waited for the first aircraft to appear. The second detail was exactly the same as the first – avoiding the dust, checking them off, the long wait and then the quick spacing and landing of them all as they all seemed to appear at once and all wanted to land at once.

I watched Tom coming in and knew he was going to make a bad landing. He bounced heavily on one wheel for some reason then shot into the air again for a few feet, finally coming to a rest too solidly. I could imagine the Scottish cursing going on in the cabin, for Tom was a particularly good pilot, and prided himself on his night landings. I wonder what he's going to blame it on, I thought, for I couldn't see him admitting that it was merely that he was out of practice after being so long on Tarmac Master duties.

However he taxied in, and I saw the other in. No one had to go round again, this happened very rarely on the second detail, the pilots were extra careful, and all were far too eager to get down and into bed to make a mistake.

I was just seeing the last aircraft in when I was surprised to see Tom walking up to me. "Did you see my landing?" "Och, Aye," I mocked. "Have you had the undercarriage checked?" Tom looked down his long nose. "We'll have none of your sarcasm," he said. "What kind of bloody flare path d'ye calls it, anyway." I resented this. "It's as straight as a dye." "Aye, it might be," he drawled, "but there's a big lump in the middle of it. Did ye no see me hit it?" "I saw you touch your right wing low," I answered. But Tom wouldn't have this. "I'm telling ye there's a brick or an anthill in the middle of your flare path. I hit the damned thing. I know."

I told him that I personally, ACP, I/C Flying had checked the flare path and landing run, but he was adamant. "Will ye no inspect it wi'me, now," he asked. "Hang on, lads," I said, "There's a crazy man wants to inspect the airfield and landing run. He'll keep me up all night if we don't."

We climbed into the jeep, and went slowly passed the flares. I told him at which flare he touched down, and we shone the headlights full on the area. I was muttering about crazy Scotsmen and their whims when with a whoop he suddenly jumped out of the jeep, and yelled for us to stop. I had seen nothing, but I joined him round the front of the jeep. He was pointing at something on the ground. "What did I tell ye," he said.

And there, trundling slowly up the flare path, was a tortoise. "That's what I landed on," he was saying. "A bloody tortoise." He picked it up, and looked at me. "Ye can no trust anybody these days."

Chapter 18

The briefing for the exercise over, I walked to the tarmac with the rest of the pilots, and we went into the crew room to get our chutes from lockers, and to sign the Authorisation Book. It was the middle of the South African summer, and in that part of the country at that time of day it was hot – very hot. Our bush jackets were sticking to us as we walked down to the aircraft. Soon, we would be in the air, and at the ten thousand feet we were scheduled to fly at it would be considerably cooler.

Inside the aircraft it was like a greenhouse. I swung up my chute and climbed in and saw two pupil navigators pouring over the tiny navigation desk. Both were sweating profusely and looked as though they had been there all day.

I had not seen them at the briefing and I nodded to them as I struggled past them to my seat. I was anxious to get away because of the heat. I turned and asked them if they were all set, and they gave me the thumbs up sign. We were not carrying a wireless operator – it was unnecessary on an ordinary daylight navigation flight, and I signalled to the mechanic to start the engines immediately.

The side window nearest me was open and it was a blessed relief when the engine started and a wonderful draft of cooler, but still warm, air flowed in.

I did the preliminary cockpit check, and as there was a practise bombing exercise tagged on to the navigational exercise, I signalled to the pupils to sort it out between themselves as to who was to climb underneath the belly of the plane to remove the bomb pins – the last operation always before taxiing out.

When he climbed in again they both gave the thumbs up sign and I was please to move off – one of the first away, I saw with satisfaction.

We climbed to ten thousand feet, after setting course above the airfield at a thousand feet, but it wasn't until we were at some 6,000 feet that it became noticeably cooler. After that the temperature went down, and soon it was pleasantly cool, and at ten thousand feet quite cold. I shut the window and turned on the heater for a while.

The pupil handed me a chit. A/C 5 degrees starboard, ETA first turning point 1435. I made a slight variation and we droned happily on. I knew the route and pinpointed us along the leg. Then up came another chit. A/C 10 degrees starboard. Drift increase. I altered course again.

I watched the ground far below drifting lazily beneath us, the tiny white ribbons of main roads splashing through a cluster of toy houses to be lost in the distant heat haze. Dried up river beds like veins on the gnarled hands of mother earth plummeted from the 7,000 foot high mountains on our starboard, and stretched themselves barrenly to the sea far away on the portside.

Another chit from the navigator. Reduce airspeed 5 knots, plus a new ETA. I glanced at the airspeed which at this height would remain rather steady, and adjusted the throttles slightly. I looked out of the window again and pinpointed a small town – we were dead on course.

After an hour of steady flying the pupil handed me a chit to alter course on to the second leg, and an ETA for the second turning point. I did a steep turn to ease the monotony, and set course for the next turning point. This leg too, took an hour to fly.

I expected a chit from the pupil giving me a base ETA and very soon it came up, a little different from the flight plan that they had drawn up before we took off. Almost immediately another chit was handed to me. Sorry, sergeant, it read. Must go to the toilet. Without turning I indicated to the door with my thumb, nodded, and altered the trim of the aircraft so that we wouldn't climb as weight was moved to the back.

I felt a tap on the shoulder, and when I looked round one of the pupils was standing there shaking his head, and rubbing his stomach. I too shook my head – there were no facilities for that sort of thing and I certainly didn't want him falling out the door with his trousers down.

He handed me another chit. URGENT. His face was now a deadly yellow, and I could see that the poor fellow was in agony. I wondered why this sort of emergency – clearly a foreseeable one and one that needed swift action – had never come up before. I resolved to ask the station medical officer what was to be done in such cases. Try not to think about it, I wrote.

He slumped to the floor, and I knew I had to do something. The other pupils' eyes boggled, and I quickly shouted at him to work out a course and ETA for base. I re-trimmed the aircraft, had a good look around the sky, and then got out of my seat. I rolled the pupil over. He opened his eyes and rolled them upwards, making violent clutches at his stomach. I shouted to him that we were going back to base, at which he just writhed and gritted his teeth.

I went back to my seat, and the other pupil handed me another chit. It read, I think he wants to spend a penny. This anti climax was too much and I wrote sarcastically, No, its appendicitis. And then the horror struck me. It was appendicitis.

I turned round and flapped my hand at the navigator who was staring at his friend as though he had also got the plague, and shouted for the alteration of course to base that I had asked for.

He worked feverishly at his board for a few moments, and then tired of waiting I turned to an approximate course, and altered the throttles so that we would lose height whilst maintaining the same airspeed. I gave this alteration to the navigator, informing him to log it, and to carry out the rest of the alterations and changes of speed as though we were still doing the exercise. Meanwhile the other pupil lay inert on the floor, and now and again gave a heart rendering twitch which convinced me that my diagnosis was correct – this was bad enough – I only hoped it was nothing worse.

As we lost height I kept a wary eye on the patient, watching for any signs of worsening of his condition, but he seemed quite content to lie there, now and again shifting his position and rolling his eyes heavenwards. He other navigator handed me a slip up eventually with his calculated alteration of course. I turned slightly, and glanced at the altimeter. We were down to 6,000 feet now, and it was becoming noticeably warmer, so I switched off the heater.

The appendicitis case rolled around on the floor a little, and then as I turned to watch him, I was amazed to see him suddenly sit bolt upright. He grinned, gave me the thumbs up sign, and the colour rushed back into his face in an incredible surge. Quickly I scribbled on the pad, 'what the devil are you up to?' He looked at the note, grinned, and once more put his thumbs up. He grabbed my pencil, and wrote on a chit. He handed it to me. It bore the one word: Wind! As an afterthought, he wrote 'had cabbage for lunch'.

He looked the picture of youthful happiness and I presumed that the decrease in pressure as we descended had relieved the pressure on his stomach. I opened the window as a precaution.

We were now only half an hour from base and flying at some 5,000 feet up the valley. I wondered whether to risk climbing again and finish off the exercise, but I couldn't have again stood the sight of the pupil writhing on the floor of the aircraft. Clearly we couldn't go straight back to base without completing something.

I wrote down, 'we shall have to complete the bombing practise, are you ok?' He nodded, and wrote down, 'what shall we put in the log?' I resisted the temptation to write 'strong winds. Unable to complete exercise', deciding that the joke wouldn't go down very well, and told him to let me have the log and I would think of something.

After a few moments I decided that there were two alternatives. Firstly we could go back to base after completing the bombing, and log the exercise as being unfinished because of the navigator's disposition, which would entail a medical for him and an inquest for me, or we could cook the log, with no one the wiser.

I decided on the latter course, and by shouting and writing down on the eternal chits the best way to do this they cooked a reasonable log between them while I stooged the aircraft round the hills to lose time.

I asked what ETA bombing range they had worked out, and when this was given I took the aircraft slowly to bombing height, and headed towards the range which was only a few miles from base. It was quite a relief to be able to fl without having to watch airspeed too meticulously, and to have to fly on a dead accurate course. There was no feeling of fatigue, and I decided that this was how all flying should be.

As we climbed I watched the pupil anxiously for any signs of a recurrence of his symptoms, but each time he waved cheerily and grinned. Soon we were over the bombing range and we were the first aircraft there. I told them to go easy and that we would do a dummy run. I didn't want any questions asked as to why we were back so early.

We did the bombing slowly and on the final run up to the target I was pleased to see other aircraft buzzing round now waiting impatiently for their turn on the range.

Soon we were losing height over the base, and in no time joined the circuit. I told the navigator who had not had any wind trouble to wind down the undercarriage, and the other pupil I asked to make a quick but thorough check of his log.

We landed, and got out to the stifling dusty hear of late afternoon. I hoped that I was not on night flying, I had had enough for one day. The pupils walked ahead of me towards their flight huts. I caught up with them, and asked if they were ok. They were laughing about it now and discussing the episode rather crudely, but stopped as I reached them.

"By the way," I said, "you'd better see that all those chits are burned. They would give the game away." Their faces dropped. "But we thought you had them, Sergeant…" "Didn't you pick them up?" I shouted.

They both shook their heads dumbly, and I could cheerfully have taken them to 10,000 feet and left them there. "They must still be in the kite," I mumbled, "Go on, off you go - I'll get them." I walked back to the aircraft, but it had been cleaned out quickly and there was not a chit to be seen.

I searched the tarmac for the native cleaner. After showing me his teeth for a long minute he remembered giving the chits to an aircraftman. I bullied him into finding him for me. The aircraftman said that he had given them to a corporal. "Orders," he said. I asked what would corporal do with them, he shrugged, he was neither interested nor civil. I asserted my authority and told him to put his cap on, but he just grinned and walked away.

I went to the fitter's hut but the corporal there had not had the chits, and he suggested that they'd be dumped in the rubbish chit by now. I decided not to bother about it - they had probably been dumped. I was hot, thirsty, and walked wearily back to the mess.

After washing I joined some of the other in the mess ante room. We looked at the night flying lists. I was detailed for two sessions, and was horrified to see that my first pair of pupils was the ones I had just been with.

But worse was to come. I had just taken my seat at dinner when a sergeant fitter sidled up to me. "You were flying King Charlie this afternoon, weren't you?" I nodded, wondering what part of his precious airframe I had broken. "I thought so," he said, "I just wanted to make sure." "Why?" I asked, and then I realised. This was the man who wrote the tittle tattle page for the station magazine. "You wouldn't. You couldn't use those chits?" I asked heavily. "I could," he said, "and will," and promptly disappeared.

I t didn't come as much of a surprise after that, when I got a big helping of cabbage for my dinner.

Chapter 19

It had been long my proud boast that I had never seen the inside of an Air Force sick-bay, nor had I ever reported sick. Then disaster overtook me and I feared I should be invalided out when I had to report sick twice in one week.

The first was for a simple but painful thing – I was on early morning flying, and being roused early I always half dressed while lying on the bed, before dragging myself to the showers. I could never bear to wander around naked at that early hour as most others did who were on the detail. This morning I reached to the floor for my socks, and felt a splinter from the wood floor tearing into the flesh behind a thumb nail. I hopped out bed quicker than I have ever done before and let out a howl that woke everyone in the billet. About two inches of wood stuck out from my nail, and when I pulled it, it broke off just below the inside of the nail leaving a good half inch embedded.

It was agonising, and though I cut the nail down and probed at the splinter, it wouldn't budge.

I showed it to Bill Tranter who was also on early flying, but all I from him was pure sarcasm as he ambled off to the shower. I decided to leave it and have another go when I had finished the morning's flying. It never occurred to me, then, to go to the sick bay; there wasn't that much time for that anyway if I wanted breakfast as well.

I sucked my thumb during the whole of the flight, and by the time we landed it was throbbing and swollen, and I immediately made for the sick-bay. There was an orderly on duty, a cross-eyed LAC, who took one look at it, and grunted. "Looks bad. What is it?"

I explained that it was a wood splinter. He eyes straightened for a fleeting moment, and he rubbed his hands together. "Good," he said, "We'll have to operate." "Who?" "Me," he said. I asked him where the MO was, but he didn't reply.

He started humming, and gathering basins together, and then led me into a small room that smelled of strong antiseptic, which was enough to unnerve me at the best of times. He sat me down, and then donned a white overall. "The butcher, they call me," he said happily. "Look here," I protested, "have you ever done this before?"

He paused for a moment, looked at me, and said quietly, "No. Have you?" which I thought was a fair enough answer, and watched him as he boiled some water with obvious fiendish delight. He still hummed as he poured some permanganate of potash crystals into a dish. "This is just to soften up the flesh," he explained.

When the water boiled he poured it on to the crystals. "Stick your thumb in there," he said. I rose from the chair. "Not on your life." "Aircrew," he murmured, "they're always the softest." He looked down his long sharp nose with those awful eyes, and went on, "shall the butcher cool it for you?" "Well I'm certainly not going to stick it in there as it is!"

Grudgingly he held the basin under the tap and trickled a drop of cold water into it. "There you are. Stick it in, before the ice forms." It was clearly not much cooler than boiling even now, but fortunately at that moment somebody yelled for him and he dashed off, with a hurried warning, "You'd better stick it in, or I shan't do the operation."

As soon as he had gone I cooled it under the tap, sat down and put my throbbing thumb in it. It hurt badly at first, but soon felt a little soothed. The orderly came back, and before I could take evasive action he poured more boiling water into the basin. "Think I'm daft, don't you?" he said.

I howled as the heat bit into my thumb, and pulled it out immediately. "You miserable little coward," he said, gritting his teeth, and I could see he was really annoyed. "I'd like to have you in here for a week." "Who the devil do you think you're talking to?" I asked.

He snapped his fingers. "Now don't come the old rank stuff with me," he said, "I don't give that" and he snapped his fingers again, "For you, for the MO, for the CO or for the Marshall of the Air Force. Report me for insubordination and you'll be doing me a favour. Now, get your thumbs stuck in there." He started humming again, his anger apparently cooled.

I could see no further point in arguing, and stuck my thumb into the liquid. He watched my face, enjoying the torture on my face. I held it there for some time, every now and again he would top it up with boiling water, until there was eventually no pain in my thumb, nor feeling. "You live in a torture chamber?" I asked him.

He hummed and took no notice of my idle chatter. Then he took my thumb out, and with a long pair of scissors he sliced down the nail with one quick movement. He probed for a moment, and then fished out the splinter. "There," he said, "didn't hurt a bit, did it?" I had to admit it didn't. "I like operations best," he said, "but now we shall have to dress it. Follow me."

I followed him, and he took me into another room where he dressed the wound expertly. "I should come again, and let the quack see it," he suggested. I left him murmuring that I would certainly not see him again.

Two days later I was back, and in the middle of the night. I saw the same orderly again. "I'm reporting special sick," I said, "and demand to see the MO." "Oh. And what's the trouble?" "Boil." "Where?" "Groin." He smiled. "That's unusual. Let's have a look." I refused.

Patiently he promised not to touch or meddle. All he wanted was to see it, in order that he may make sure whether it was important enough to wake the MO. "Is there no MO on duty, then?" I asked. "Not tonight. Only the butcher." "Right." I said, "I'll come back in the morning."

I went back to my billet and spent a restless night – the boil; huge, uncomfortable and embarrassing was on the point of bursting.

When I saw the MO in the morning, he ordered me to get some kit and move into the sick-bay straight away. I demurred, and asked that I may be an outpatient only, but he said to do as he asked, if I would be good enough so there was no option.

I trudged wearily back to the billet for shaving kit and pyjamas, full of trepidation as to my fate in the hands of the cross-eyed, would-be, surgeon. "I'd like to have you here for a week," he had said only two days before. I felt like deserting.

Johnny was in the billet, and he laughed fit to drop when I told him what had happened. "I'll come and visit you," he said, and when I thanked him, he replied that it was only that he'd like to see this butcher character in action. He gave me a book to read while I was in there. I looked at the title. It was Dale Carnegie's, "How to Win Friends and Influence People."

The orderly sneered when he saw me in bed. "Aircrew," he snarled, "are the softest of His Majesty's Fighting Services. No wonder we're losing the war."

I asked him whose side he was on. "Nobody's," he replied. "I'm an absolute pacifist. A conscientious objector who was forced into looking after spineless little mother's darlings like yourself." He whipped back the clothes from the bed. "Lets' have a look at this boil." He fetched a basin and water, and I feared the worst. I protested, but he explained gleefully, "Orders from the quack. Now shut up and lie still while I squeeze it."

I groaned as he swabbed and pressed and squeezed and would cheerfully have murdered the man, but he was amazingly strong, and with one of his elbows in my chest and the rest of his weight distributed about me like a strait-jacket I was helpless. When he'd finished pulverising the boil he straightened up, gave me a tablet and a glass of water. "That's your lot, now. Two tablets later in the day, one tonight. You're on a diet."

"No food?" I asked incredulously. "No food," he repeated. "Quack's orders." "Would you please stop calling the MO quack," I shouted.

He looked down his skinny nose. "Tut, tut," he smiled, "we are sensitive, aren't we? You really shouldn't have joined, you know. Such a rough crowd of boys."

If I could've stood he would have been floored. I lay back on the bed staring miserably out of the window, and hoped that the MO would be around soon. I felt perfectly fit, and so absolutely useless lying there. But he didn't come, I never saw him all the time I was on and had rely far too much on the cross-eyed fanatic.

The next morning two new patients arrived. One was an RAF officer who had been on the same course that I had been on at SFTS. He walked casually in, hands in pockets, and stood staring out of the window, "What on earth is the matter with you?" I asked him.

He was strikingly good looking, blond and lean, and reminded me always of those handsome chaps they dig up for advertising "Fly with RAF". But today he looked downright miserable, and at that moment I had no idea he was a patient. He turned and looked morosely at me. "Haven't you heard?"

I shook my head waiting for him to carry on. "I thought everybody had," he continued. "I pranged in when landing today. Stuck the under cart up through the fuselage." "Anybody hurt?" "No." "Then it's not so bad. A court of inquiry will soon clear that up," I said. "How did it happen?" "Oh," he answered off-handily, "just piled in, that's all. One of those things. I'm glad it happened. I hate flying those damned things." "Who doesn't? But somebody has to do it. For some it's worse than being on ops, for others better. We might be on ops one day." I stopped myself, realising that I was talking like a Dutch uncle.

I was amazed to see him trembling. "I'll never go on ops. I'll never fly again. I've always hated it, right from Grading School. Hated every single minute. How I ever got through I don't know. I'm posted back to Blighty now, and I'm glad." "You!" I gasped.

He nodded. "Seven hundred hours in my log book, and I've loathed every second. Sweated on every trip. My god, what should I have done on ops?"

The conversation was proving a little embarrassing to us both and I was glad when the cross-eyed monster called him to go to see the MO. I didn't see him again, and never heard what did eventually happen. Word just went round that he had been posted and that was it.

The same afternoon an airman was moved into the sickbay. He was lying on his stomach on a wheeled stretcher escorted by the orderly. "Company for you. He's had his arse chopped off with a propeller, so you can swap stories about your wounds." The man half crawled and was half pushed onto the bed by the orderly He lay quietly on his stomach.

As soon as the orderly had gone I hobbled over to him and offered him a cigarette. He told me that he had been guiding in a taxiing aircraft, and had walked into the airscrew of one that was parked. "It sliced my behind like a bacon slicer," he said, without smiling, "I thought I was a goner." "Could have been worse – but not much," I said, sympathetically. "It is worse," he said.

I paused, waiting for him to tell me the rest. "As soon as I'm up I'm to be put on a charge for negligence." That was indeed worse, but there was still more. "Troubles always come in threes," he said. "I'm on a posting list for blighty next week." "Which you've had," I smiled. "You could never stand up all the way there." He agreed sadly, and fell asleep, the cigarette still between his fingers.

I went back to bed, and the orderly came in. He sniffed. "You've been smoking." "No, I've been sleeping," I lied. "I dreamed that you had remustered, and you were guiding in my taxiing aircraft…" "The butcher will never re-muster," he said. "Now, let's have a look at that boil."

Chapter 20

The first trip after languishing in sick-bay for three days was a low flying exercise. All pilots turned up for this exercise, three were never any with 'colds' or 'strained backs', or even 'boils'. We had one of these every month, and along with a Sea Sweep was the most popular of exercises.

The navigation was mostly done by low level pinpointing, not as easy, by any means, as navigating from a height, which meant that the pupils were on their toes the whole time. Most pupils dreaded these exercises, for the trip was usually bumpy, they were busy, it was hot, and it was one trip on which all the pilots – except those that wouldn't buy a drink in the mess and were known as poor types – let their hair down, (unofficially) and flew at full throttle as low as they dare, and in complete disregard for the pupil's flight plans, which on many occasions had to be cooked.

On the way down to the flights with Johnny and Ken I met the fearless Scotsman, Tom, who was now hogging the hours as much as he possibly could in order to make up for lost time as Tarmac Master.

"How about a wee bit of low flying formation?" he asked us. "You've a nasty habit of coming in at people's back doors," said Kenny. "No thanks." "I would, but I can't ride a bike," I explained, and Johnny mumbled something about a film at the local cinema that he hoped to live long enough to see. "Och, I'm a wee bit unpopular," said the man from Fife, "but I'll be on the lookout for you lads. Don't say I didn't warn ye."

As we signed the Authorisation Book I made a note of Tom's aircraft number, and decided that if he did come in close I would give him a run for his money. He loved formation flying but was finding it increasingly difficult to find partners, and although there was certainly justification for constant refusals I considered the risk now negligible – Tom had learned his lesson.

I told the pupils to watch out for his aircraft, and went forward to start up. Before I could attract the attention of a mechanic to swing the airscrews the timekeeper from the flight office ran over and signalled to me. I opened my window, and asked her what the matter was. She explained that we had to change aircraft. "Is this U/S?" I asked. "No, someone else is taking it," she cried out. "Your flight has been re-authorised."

We left the aircraft and I went back to the flight office. I looked to see who was taking my aircraft but although my name was scratched out no one else had been put in. Things like this happened now and again, it was of no consequence, and so I signed the re-authorisation, and went to search for the other aircraft. It was at the top of the tarmac, always a bad place to get a mechanic to start one up; they didn't like walking so far.

However I managed to attract the attention of one eventually and unhurriedly he started me up. I taxied out behind a line of others noticing that I'd be one of the last to get off.

In the air I climbed to 7,000 feet above the airfield, and set course directly over the mountains which seemed from this height to skirt the edge of the airfield. After a few minutes I began losing height. There were a few chunks of cumulus cloud over the mountains, and, descending to their level I weaved in and out, studying the tops of the crusty mountains, their jutting peaks, gulleys and sharp black shadows thrusting the delicate greens and blues into glaring relief. The mountains, when we were near enough to study detail, always fascinated me. This was flying at its most delicious.

We flew down the other side of the mountain, ruggedly beautiful in the morning sun, and turning so that we were on a parallel course to the range we were soon looking up at them instead of down.

At a thousand feet I levelled out, and turned away from the hills looking out for the small landmark from which we would descend to low level and set course. I looked back at the pupils. They were both sitting quietly playing pocket draughts. I pulled the aeroplane up in a vicious climbing turn, pulled back the throttles, and as she almost stood on her tail I pushed the stick forward, and into a fairly steep dive. I looked back. The pupils were still playing draughts, but they had to hang on.

They glared as I signalled for them to start the exercise, and with an air of complete boredom they shuffled their navigation papers. I gave them the thumbs up sign as I straightened out a few feet above the ground and saw the pinpoint starting place sweep beneath us.

I had already told them to tap me on the shoulder as soon as they had speed, drifts and courses under control, so that I might descend to ground level and concentrate on low flying rather than on watching air speed and course. When I felt the tap, I set the gyro indicator, meaning to glance at it only occasionally, and throttled back a little. We descended, until the ground immediately in front was just a confused blur, and I put on more throttle, holding them with one hand, my other firmly on the stick, moving it, sometimes gently, sometimes fiercely, but moving it all the time as we flew the contours of the ground below. This was the only time we had any impression at all of speed, and we all made the most of it.

Houses and huts flashed beneath us – a pull back on the stick and we cleared them by what seemed mere inches, and then an immediate push down on the stick and a straightening out again. Sometimes the occupants ran out shaking their fists as their sheep or fowl or dogs took fright, and often natives threw themselves flat convinced that their end had come. We didn't frighten them purposely, and I always avoided doing so as far as possible, but human nature being what it is; the thrill came first, regrets and conscience afterwards.

We flashed across a dried up river bed, and I turned to follow it weaving along between the banks, throttling back and forth gently turning, sometimes skid turning or a steep turn when the aircraft seemed to stand on one wing tip only inches from the ground, and then the tendency is to increase it, to heel over more.

I levelled out, and turned quickly to see if the pupils were enjoying it. They weren't, but at least they weren't playing draughts. I flew on the approximate flight plan course again and climbed a little to have a look around. Ahead I saw two aircraft, one creeping up on the other. I wondered if Tom was after a bit of formation flying, and opening the throttle I moved forward slowly narrowing the gap until I could see the registration letters. The rear aircraft was Tom, and a little later I could see that the one in front was the one I was originally to take.

Tom, of course, would think that he was creeping up on me, and I only hoped that it was someone who wouldn't suddenly panic if they caught sight of another aeroplane out of the corner of their eye – this can be very disturbing when not expected.

I watched them for a while flying behind at a discreet distance, and a little higher than we had been flying. Tom closed in slowly, and soon tucked himself well into the other aircraft, so that his wing tip was between the main-plane and tail-plane of the leading aircraft. This was not near enough for Tom apparently who closed in even more, so that his wing tip was now almost touching the door. He used to say that he knock at the door of an aircraft in flight. I now believed him, but wished that he wouldn't go quite so close on low level.

I could imagine Tom sitting there grinning trying to attract the attention of the pilot, believing it to be me. I thought it might be a good idea to close in on him, when suddenly he made a steep upward turn, and sped away, soon to be lost against the blurring ground. The other pilot must have seen him and waved him away, for he just carried on at the same height and airspeed.

We turned on to the second leg of our flight on the ETA that the navigators had worked out. This was a short leg and I flew it at a constant speed and course in order that they might put their log in order. We lost the other aircraft, too, as we turned. Either we, or they, were out in their timing.

On the third leg I went down to ground level again, climbing only to change over the fuel tank, and then descending again. We came across a herd of animals that appeared from nowhere, and as we passed overhead they darted about in a mad frenzy, colliding with each other and getting bowled over in their rush to escape the noise.

I followed a roadway for some time. In the far distance I could see a cloud of dust which suggested a vehicle of some kind. When we reached it, it turned out to be a smart American car, huge and fast, and a female's head popped out of the side window, as we flew over. The second navigator shouted that I could drop him there, and I was glad to see that he had at least noticed something.

Soon it was time to climb again, slightly without altering the airspeed, and then as we pinpointed our starting point we climbed more steeply gaining the few thousand feet we needed to get over the mountains. We seemed to be hardly moving now after the last two hours at low level and as we got into smoother air and higher we seemed to be hovering.
The navigators settled down to their draughts again and I wondered whether I should be night flying. If I was it was at least better than lying in a sick-bay with very little wrong with me.

While stacking the parachutes in the lockers there were the usual line shoots. There were those who had been so low that the pitot head had been bent or got sand in, there were those who had to endorse the Form 700 "Propellers bent at tips", and there were those who leaned out of the door and picked wild flowers. The prize I thought went to the intrepid one who, flying up a river bed with water in it (a line-shoot in itself) flew so low that his altimeter read in fathoms.

I looked out for Tom. He didn't appear to be there, and I asked Johnny and Ken if he had formatted on them. They shook their heads, and with a smile Ken said, "I only hope he formatted on the OC flying!" "Why, was Major Goodson flying?" I asked. "He's down in the book," said Ken. "Didn't he take your aeroplane?" "Good lord," I exclaimed, "was he flying that?"

I told them of seeing Tom practising his very tight formation and decided that we had better look for him, and tell him before the major got hold of him. He could at least work out some alibi if he wasn't taken unawares. In all probability Tom would have this well worked out by now if he had recognised Major Goodson.

He came into the crew room and flung his chute down. He grinned sheepishly when he saw us. "I thought you were flying Abel Baker," he said to me. "I've boobed, man." "You're not kidding," Ken replied, "do you know who was in it?" Tom shook his head. "Some SAAF Lieutenant, but I didn't recognise him. I was just going to have a look at him when he waved me away. Och, I think he was a wee bit cross."

Tom was shaken badly when we told him who it was. "Tell him it wasn't you. Tell him you were doing a Sea sweep," Johnny said, "In error."
"Tell him you were having trouble with your eyes and didn't see him"
"Shoot him before he shoots you."
"Go sick," I said, "Go hide in the sick-bay until old Goodson forgets."
"Put in for a compassionate posting"
"Take poison."
"Re-muster."
"Resign."

We all ran out of suggestions. "Can you no realise," Tom said seriously, "that this is the second time I've done unauthorised formation flying. He's bound to take a poor view. Last time it was four weeks Tarmac Master on that blasted Yellow bike. God alone knows what it will be this time." "And he is just about to tell you!" said a voice from the doorway. "We looked round. It was Flight Lieutenant Manners, O/C A Flight. "Report to him straight away, McTavish." Tom, whose name wasn't McTavish, ambled off with a sigh.

Minutes later he was back, his face longer than ever. "Another blasted four weeks Tarmac Master." "Yellow bike an' all?" "No," he grunted, "this time on me two poor feet. Next time he says I'm to do it naked." "Oh, cor blimey," said Johnny, "who does he think he's punishing next time?"

Chapter 21

We were all sorry the following weekend when all the available pilots were detailed to fly the football team and supporters to an Air School three or four hundred miles away, and we had to leave Tom, an ardent fan, behind.

He waved us off cursing his luck, his beetle brows crashed together in anger as aircraft after aircraft moved off the tarmac leaving his with the prospect of very bleak weekend in camp.

The weather was good, we carried two navigator pupils and a wireless operator, for the flight was also to be an exercise, and as many passengers as could wangle their way aboard. The aircraft had no seats for passengers and they settled themselves on the main spar, on the floor, on the pupil's table, and around the wireless operator's equipment, getting in the way but doing their best. To ease the crush in our aircraft I stood one lanky corporal with his head into the astro-dome and told him to keep a lookout, and another I stuck in the nose and prayed that he wouldn't be sick.

Winding the undercarriage up was an ordeal, there just wasn't the room and it was a particularly stiff one, so we were about halfway there when the pale and perspirating airman straightened himself and gave me the thumbs up sign, and mouthed the words, "its up". At least, I think those were the words he mouthed.

The aircraft was heavy on the controls and a good deal slower with all this crew aboard, and as there was a head wind progress was slow. It was an old aircraft, too, and it seemed that if I gave her engines maximum boost she would just fly above stalling speed. I didn't dare to think what would happen when we eventually put flap down and increased drag even more. First things first, however, we had to get there.

Now and again we spotted another Anson in our vicinity, and once we passed head on a civil airline Dakota on its way to Capetown. The passengers in our aircraft pressed themselves to every window to wave at the Dakota, and we could see the passenger's faces at the windows, wondering no doubt how many people could get into a little plane. The pilots just looked at us, noses in the air; they seemed to resent our presence in their air.

When we were about an hour's flying time from our destination I saw what appeared to be a puff of smoke or dust in the distance, and the same time the corporal with his head in the astro-dome noticed it, for he passed me a chit which read, "Crow's nest to Bridge. Smoke astern. Otherwise, all quiet."

I asked the wireless operator over the intercom if he could find any music, but he wasn't plugged in, for there was no reply. I passed a chit down asking him to plug in, but back came the reply via dozen mouths that the intercom was u/s. I stretched round to see if I could see him signal, but his headset was clamped firmly on his head and his eyes were closed. I decided to leave him, he was there in any case just for the trip, and because we were carrying passengers.

The two pupils meanwhile were busy, or appeared to be, and now and again chits came up for an alteration of course or a new ETA passed along by eager helping hands. The passengers just sat or squatted, tired now of shouting to each other. Some were reading, but all were looking cramped and uncomfortable. Presently another chit came my way. It was from the wireless operator, and judging from the condition of the paper it had been passed from hand to hand and digested. It explained the smoke in the distance.

It appeared that the airfield was on fire, and instructed us to wait for landing instructions. Now everyone craned forward and crowded up front so that the tri of the aircraft had to be altered. The smoke now was thick and black, and it obscured most of the town and all of the Air School. As we got nearer it was obvious that it absolutely impossible to land, and there were many gloomy faces at the thought of a football match that wouldn't come off.

I thought that we might be diverted to another Air School in the vicinity, for none of us would have enough fuel to return to base. However there was plenty of time to decide about that, for we were still far enough away from the fire to have burnt itself out by the time we got there.

When we were almost over the airfield – I planned to circle around on leeside – the airman form the bomb aimer's compartment started to wriggle himself from his cramped and uncomfortable position. Two of his friends saw him struggling, and yanked him out by his ankles. He looked pale, and I thought he was going to be sick. He struggled towards me, and cupped his hand round my ear, and shouted so that my ear drum almost burst, "There's a lot of smoke down there!"

I shook my head, and shouted back to him, in a rather smart-arse manner, that it wasn't smoke – merely Scotch mist, and not to worry.

With a grin the lanky young airman wriggled back into the nose, and I followed another aircraft into a circuit of the field. Ahead one or two aircraft were weaving about despite warnings from the R/T to keep away from the immediate vicinity of the airfield.

Almost half the airfield seemed to be on fire, now – thickly tufted brown grass fanned by a seemingly stiffish breeze blazed merrily towards the hangars and I could see frenzied little figures pushing toy aeroplanes away from the path of the flames and onto the perimeter.

We had a grandstand view of hurrying figures, small dashing fire tenders and minute cars aligning themselves along the fringe of the fire, and immense puffs of smoke rising suddenly where the flames were beaten or trodden or soused with water or sand. And still it seemed to be advancing, and I could see little hope of our landing there that day.

I asked the wireless operator to query whether we should divert to another airfield, but I got the cryptic reply that it was the airfield that was ablaze, not the soccer field, and would I please stay away from the vicinity of the airfield and await instructions. The wireless operator – a keen soccer fan – bubbled with joy as he passed back the message.

I drew up to the starboard side of the aircraft in front, and flew alongside. He waved me in. I was pleased to see that it was Ken. He pointed down, and shrugged. I shrugged back at him. He leaned over to his starboard window, across the lap of a frightened looking LAC and drew out the letters EL on the window followed by a question mark. I grinned back, and mouthed, "Yes, please." To land in East London instead of this inland school with a raging bush fire would have pleased us both.

I drew away a little and looked to see how the fire was progressing. There seemed to be little change, and as the aircraft was becoming hot at this fairly low altitude and the sun was directly ahead, I decided to climb a little to cool off.

As I climbed, the lanky one from the bomb aimer's compartment struggled backwards and out again. He grabbed my shoulder, and shouted, much too loudly, that he as sure it was smoke. I goggled at him, and wondered who was kidding whom.

Presently, at about ten thousand feet another airman tapped me and asked could he take over. He explained that he had fifty hours on Oxford's and had been washed out, but he could certainly manage straight and level. He was a cool looking individual, and more out of sympathy than anything else I climbed from the seat, and held the aircraft straight and level as he got in. I looked around at all the glum faces. They were all sitting cramped up, most of them unable even to see out, and had been so now for almost three hours. It was impossible for them to move around, and too much of an effort to carry on a normal conversation above the noise of the engines.

I wrote out a chit explaining that I was sorry they couldn't smoke, but if they did would they do it in twos, and pass up the doused cigarette ends in a match box that I may count them. I had had to explain cigarette ends away before, and though smoking was forbidden in the Anson, and was in fact foolish, there are times when the risks are justified, and the poor travellers looked as though they were ready to be blown into eternity anyway. I, too, lit a cigarette, and was pleased to see that only one other man did – the others would wait their turn. I watched the new pilot handle the aircraft, and signalled to him to turn to port slowly. He did a perfect turn, and levelled the nose up again on the airfield ahead.

We flew backwards and forwards like this for half an hour while everyone drew on lady nicotine, and dutifully handed up their cigarette ends in a matchbox. I counted them, and deducted two – one for the man who was flying and the other for the chap in the nose – I daren't risk hauling him out and asking if he cared for a smoke.

All the aircraft had by this time arrived and were droning over the airfield at varying heights and speeds. There was still no diversion from the ground, and I realised that now we should all have to land; there was no-one with enough fuel to go further a field.

I lost height again to have a closer look, keeping my eyes peeled for other aircraft; one never knew what the pilots might be doing to relieve the monotony. It seemed that, although the fire was still bad, it was under control. The town fire brigade was there, too, and the organised beating seemed to be having some effect. There was now more smoke than fire.

A voice eventually crackled through the intercom, telling us to sort ourselves out and land – in ones, and as far to the farthest side of the airfield as possible. Beware sparks and burning tufts, we were warned, and taxi quickly round the perimeter track once in.

The circus started. Everyone dived into the circuit at the same time, and aircraft were flying almost nose to tail in the circuit, being jostled out of the queue where there was the slightest possibility. I clung to the aircraft in front as closely as I dared, giving not an inch – had I done so I would have been pushed to the back, as the aircraft behind – very closely behind, was waiting for a quick jump in. I guessed he was going to try and cut me in a turn, and fooled him by losing a few feet of height and passing beneath him.

It was inevitable that some aircraft had to go round again. But it is also unbelievable that we were all inside a quarter of an hour. The smell of the burning turf was everywhere, and as we drew level with the burned up patch we could see that the fire was far from out. Over half the field was smouldering, and part of the other half was breaking out in small flurries of flame, only to be quickly attacked by a car or jeep full of airmen, or if it was a thick flare up, a squirt from the end of a fireman's hose.

Everyone was talking excitedly as we walked from the planes, all swapping experiences. We considered that the Air Force Medal was the least that could be offered for a safe landing on a blazing airfield.

I walked from the tarmac, having signed the book, and towards the mess with Ken and Johnny, when suddenly from an open window a voice bellowed, "You—Sergeant!"

We all stopped. The message was obviously meant for one of us, but which one we didn't know. We were all Sergeants. We soon knew. A stick pointed from the window at me, and behind the stick a formidable looking warrant officer.

"You. Come here." "Blimey," said Ken. "The S.W.O. See you in the mess." He and Johnny moved over, as I made my way to the office.

I knocked timidly, and the voice bade me to enter. He was standing hands on hips, stick clenched resolutely. He looked me up and down. "No hat!" he screamed, "Where's your hat?" His face grew crimson with rage as I juggled with my side cap that had been stuffed in the shoulder tabs of my battle dress. I stood to attention and listened to a lengthy tirade which I gather summed me up as being not only the dirtiest Sergeant in the Union of South Africa, but the poorest specimen of manhood that he had ever clapped his perishing eyes on, and believe him that was saying a lot. Without delay he intimated that I needed a good scrubbing over with the strongest carbolic, a shearing so that my flaming tabs might be seen (this I interpreted as needing a haircut), a clean shirt, clean underwear, clean socks, polished shoes instead of these creepers, and proper regulation length shorts.

The Air School I was from was a disgrace allowing people like me to inhabit its sergeants' mess and it was time that I was back in Civvy Street.

Eventually he urged me to go forth heeding his words of wisdom that I may not stray again, and that I may one day be the sort of chap that His Majesty would be proud to have in his Air Force.

His words were encouragement indeed as only a few hours before I had been told that I had been recommended to hold one of His Majesties' commissions.

On the way to the Mess I wondered whether I should perhaps have mentioned this to the Warrant Officer. And I hoped that the other half of his airfield would burn up – after we had taken off.

John's Photos

Pilot Officer Noble

A collection of photos: Learning as a cadet, Kessel Bay and Oudtshoorn, The locals from the train, The Gang

Getting his wings, With the gang again, A very pretty young nurse, RAF
Christmas greetings!

John's log book and final entry

John with future wife Valerie Looch.

ABOUT THE AUTHOR

Dominic Butler, grandson of John Noble, took the decision in 2010 to write up his grandfather's memoirs. He is a keen military historian, a graduate of Salford University's Military History programme and has aspirations of becoming an author and professional historian. Currently he works as an Assistant Curator at the Lancashire Infantry Museum and is writing a history-based novel.

Printed in Great Britain
by Amazon

33032621R00076